The celebrated film director François Truffaut once famously observed that there was a certain incompatibility between the terms British and cinema. That was typical of the critical disparagement for so long suffered by British films. As late as 1969 a respected film scholar could dub British cinema 'the unknown cinema'. This was the situation because up to that time the critics, scholars and intellectuals writing about cinema preferred either continental films or latterly Hollywood to the homegrown product. Over the past thirty years that position has changed dramatically. There are now books, journals, courses and conferences entirely devoted to British cinema and a wider audience for British films, now cess. screen, on video and DVD.

The Tauris British Film Guide serie   to add to that process of revaluation by assessing in depth   British   om the past hundred years. The series will draw on a'   all   nd will over time build into a wide-ranging library   with, readable books on the films that have defined Briti   ing project that will comprehensively refute Truffaut   a d demonstrate the variety, creativity, humanity   of the best of British cinema.

JEFFR
General Edito

THE BRITISH FILM GUIDE 8

The Private Life of Henry VIII

GREG WALKER

I.B. TAURIS

LONDON · NEW YORK

Published in 2003 by I.B.Tauris & Co. Ltd
6 Salem Road, London W2 4BU
175 Fifth Avenue, New York NY 10010
www.ibtauris.com

In the United States of America and Canada distributed by Palgrave
Macmillan, a division of St Martin's Press, 175 Fifth Avenue, New York
NY 10010

ISBN 1 86064 909 2

A full CIP record for this book is available from the British Library
A full CIP record for this book is available from the Library of Congress

Library of Congress catalog card: available

Set in Monotype Fournier and Univers Black by Ewan Smith, London
Printed and bound in Great Britain by MPG Books, Bodmin

Contents

Illustrations

Plates 2 and 4 are reproduced by courtesy of the National Portrait Gallery, London. Plate 6 appears courtesy of The Royal Collection © Her Majesty Queen Elizabeth II, 2002. All stills from *The Private Life of Henry VIII*, including the cover image, appear courtesy of BFI Collections and London Films Ltd, and CTE (Carlton) Ltd.

Acknowledgements

This book was written thanks to an Arts and Humanities Research Board research leave award and a sabbatical from the University of Leicester. It was completed during the first weeks of a Leverhulme Trust Major Research Fellowship. Needless to say, I am deeply grateful to all three organisations for their generosity in funding my work, and pleased to be able to record my thanks here. As someone new to the discipline, I am very grateful to those specialists in cinema history and film studies who generously shared their time and expertise with me in matters great and small. Like anyone working on Alexander Korda, I have benefited immeasurably from being able to read the comprehensive biography written by Karol Kulik, the earlier, briefer life by Paul Tabori, and Michael Korda's moving and insightful study of the Korda brothers, *Charmed Lives.* Without them I would literally not have known where to start. Three other books have also been greatly influential in the development of my ideas: Sarah Street's *British National Cinema*, Jeffrey Richards's *The Age of the Dream Palace*, and especially Sue Harper's magnificent *Picturing the Past: The Rise and Fall of the British Costume Film*. The extent of my debt to each will be evident from the notes.

More directly I am grateful to the staff of the British Film Institute archive and library, my colleagues Emma Parker and Martin Halliwell, and Dr David Salter of the University of Edinburgh (who kindly read the book in an early draft) for their advice and support. I am also greatly indebted to Dr Claire Jowitt of the University of Wales, Aberystwyth, Professor Tony Kushner of the University of Southampton (who provided me with reference material on anti-Semitism in the film industry), Dr Mark Rawlinson, my unofficial 'study-leave buddy', Professor Jeffrey Richards the BFG series editor, and Philippa Brewster of I.B.Tauris, each of whom read a draft of the book and offered invaluable help and guidance. Dr Stuart Ball of Leicester's History Department generously shared his knowledge of Conservative Party history with me, Miriam Gill of the Art History Department loaned me numerous books and videos, and Dr John Drew of the University of Buckingham helped track down articles. Thanks too to Michael Davies, Michael and Andy Hagiioannu, Kevin Jacklin, Anne Marie D'Arcy and George Bernard for their ongoing friendship and willingness to endure lunchtime conversations about Alexander Korda, London Films and Charles Laughton's eating habits.

Most of all, I have been able concentrate on this book thanks to the support and understanding of my wife, Sharon, and our children Matthew and David, who were prepared for a time to countenance the TV being taken over by 'awful' black-and-white films, only occasionally making their displeasure known. Similarly I could not have written this without the support of two excellent heads of department, Professor Elaine Treharne and Professor Vince Newey. The latter in particular has been a stalwart ally and benefactor, and, although he will not approve, I should like to dedicate this book to him as a token of my appreciation of all that he has done.

Foreword

Alexander Korda's masterpiece *The Private Life of Henry VIII* (London Film Productions, 1933) was probably the most important film produced in Britain before the Second World War. It is, as Jeffrey Richards has observed, 'a film which, if any does, deserves the epithet "epoch-making"', and remains, in Sue Harper's words, 'crucial in any history of British film culture'. With this one film Korda effectively 'put British pictures on the world map', and drew from Charles Laughton 'one of the most achieved performances in film history'.[1]

Until now, however, *Henry VIII* has not been the subject of a sustained critical study. This book makes good that omission, offering a detailed account of the film, its makers and its place in the cultural and cinematic history of the period. It tells the fascinating story of the film's conception and realisation, of its phenomenal critical and box-office success, and the consequences of that success for the British film industry in the 1930s. It discusses Korda's own early career and the place of *Henry VIII* in his development as a director and producer, and examines the Academy Award-winning performance of Charles Laughton in the title role.

Henry VIII is more than simply a superb film; it opens up a whole series of questions concerning the cinematic and cultural history of Britain in the 1930s. In subsequent chapters the book focuses on the film's cultural impact and implications. Through an analysis of key scenes and sequences it examines the narrative's subtle encoding of questions of Englishness and national identity, looking more widely at both the cosmopolitan nature of London Films and Korda's own complex conception and negotiation of questions of race and of national and 'international' identity. A further chapter discusses Korda's vision of the 'international film', the cinematic representation of British history, and *Henry VIII*'s use of modern stereotypes to bridge the gap between the ideas of past and present, public and private that it deploys.

Henry VIII is also more intensely political than many previous

accounts have suggested. Drawing upon evidence from the parliamentary and media debates of the period, this guide identifies the film's
engagement with the most contentious political issues of the decade:
appeasement, national defence and opposition to Continental fascism.
Placing it in the context of Korda's other highly politicised films of the
1930s and the director's connections with Winston Churchill, Brendan
Bracken and others on the die-hard wing of the Conservative Party, it
suggests greater continuities in London Films' political stance through
the period than most film historians have allowed.

Finally, the book examines the intriguing representation of gender
and sexuality in the film, not only in the portrayal of Henry's wives, but
also in the complex, problematic exploration of masculinity evident in
Charles Laughton's central performance. It suggests how the film not
only humanises Henry VIII, universalising his experience as that of the
archetypal 'henpecked husband', but also, by simultaneously infantilising
him, buys into a conventional comic strategy to deflect attention from
any of the more troubling questions that his story provokes.

Film Credits

THE PRIVATE LIFE OF HENRY VIII

Producers	Alexander Korda and Ludovico Toeplitz for London Film Productions
Distributors	United Artists
Director	Alexander Korda
Assistant Director	Geoffrey Boothby
Screenplay	Arthur Wimperis
Story	Lajos Biró and Arthur Wimperis
Cinematography	Georges Périnal
Camera Operator	Osmond Borradaile
Settings	Vincent Korda
Costume Design	John Armstrong
Costumiers	B. J. Simmons and Co.
Music	Kurt Schroeder
Sound	A.W. Watkins
Film Editing	Stephen Harrison
Editorial Supervision	Harold Young
Production Manager	David B. Cunynghame
Technical Adviser	Philip Lindsay
Choreography	Espinosa
Falconry Adviser	Captain C. W. R. Knight
Running Time	96 minutes
UK Première	24 October 1933
US Première	12 October 1933

CAST

Charles Laughton	Henry VIII
Robert Donat	Culpeper
Lady Tree	Henry's Old Nurse
Binnie Barnes	Catherine Howard
Elsa Lanchester	Anne of Cleves
Merle Oberon	Anne Boleyn

Franklin Dyall	Cromwell
Miles Mander	Wriothesley
Wendy Barrie	Jane Seymour
Claud Allister	Cornell
John Loder	Thomas Peynell
Everley Gregg	Catherine Parr
Laurence Hanray	Cranmer
William Austin	Duke of Cleves
Frederick Culley	Duke of Norfolk
Gibb McLaughlin	French Executioner
Sam Livesey	English Executioner
Wally Patch	Carver
William Heughan	Kingston
Judy Kelly	Lady Rochford
John Turnbull	Holbein

Sources, Film Credits. Additional information from the Leicester Square Theatre Opening Night Programme (BFI Archive, LFP Collection: film ephemera), and courtesy of *The Internet Movie Data Base*. Used with permission.

ONE
Origins

MAKING BRITISH HISTORY

During the early months of 1933, the émigré Hungarian film producer Alexander Korda spent a good deal of his time hosting dinner parties for financiers and industrialists in his London hotel suite, seeking backing for a somewhat implausible-sounding film project: the story of the short and unconsummated marriage of Henry VIII and Anne of Cleves. By all accounts his experience was not encouraging. As Korda later retold the story, he was at a severe disadvantage from the outset: 'The costume picture was the most disliked thing in the world. My colleagues said the public would not stand for it – they even told me it would be unwise to use King Henry's name in the title and wanted me to call the picture *The Golden Bed*.'[1] A steady stream of potential investors declined the invitation. Even Michael Balcon, the chief of production at Gaumont British Films, who had backed Korda's work before, turned his request down flat.[2]

Finally, at the second attempt, Richard Norton (later Lord Grantley), who was then representing United Artists (Korda's American distributors) in London, persuaded his American employers to provide seed-corn funding for the project. This came in the form of an advance on distribution revenues – memories differ over whether this was £15,000 or £20,000.[3] On the strength of this commitment Korda was able to begin shooting in May 1933 at the British and Dominion studios at Elstree. Only later did he persuade Ludovico Toeplitz de Grand Ry, the son of an Italian banker, to provide sufficient additional money to complete the film. So Korda went into production without the money to finish the project, and with a cast containing only one major star, Charles Laughton, who was to play King Henry. The remainder of the major roles, with the exception of Queen Anne (played by Laughton's wife, Elsa Lanchester), were taken by the stable of actors contracted to Korda's company, London Film Productions. After seven complete rewrites

(Korda was later to claim to Winston Churchill that it took twelve), the script, co-authored by the humourist Arthur Wimperis and the Hungarian playwright Lajos Biró, was expanded to include appearances by five of Henry's six wives; but Korda (after a brief flirtation with 'The Royal Husband') stuck to his reputedly unfashionable title, *The Private Life of Henry VIII*, and the whole project was wrapped up in five weeks.[4]

The rest, as they say, is history. The resulting picture was proclaimed 'the key film in the history of British cinematography' within a year of its opening, and was to have a revolutionary effect, not only on the career of its producer-director and a number of its actors, but upon the whole British film industry.[5] Estimates of precisely how much the film eventually cost to make vary from £50,000 to £93,710, but all sources agree that it went on to make over £500,000 in return for the initial investment – an unprecedented figure for a British film – and it was still earning nearly £10,000 a year from revivals in the early 1950s.[6] On its opening night in New York alone the film took £7,500 (Korda audaciously premièred the film in three cities, at New York's Radio City Music Hall on 12 October 1933, then in Paris and, subsequently, on 24 October at the Leicester Square Theatre in London, thus signalling his international ambitions), and its success with audiences and critics alike was phenomenal. The *Daily Mail* described it as the 'greatest British film triumph' to date. The *Sunday Express* declared 'it puts British films two or three years forward in one bound ... it will make British history'. The *Sydney Morning Herald* judged it 'one of the most vital, and most Rabelaisian things that have ever been placed on the screen'. C. A. Lejeune, writing in *The Picturegoer* in 1934, went further, claiming that Korda had 'done more than any other producer in the country to put British films on the map of the world'. [7]

Henry VIII is remembered today chiefly for Laughton's bravura performance in the title role, for which he won an Academy Award for Best Actor, and especially for the scene in which he sits at the dining table picking a chicken to pieces with his hands, throwing the bones over his shoulder, offering between belches a lament for the gracelessness of the age ('There's no delicacy nowadays. No consideration for others. [*Belch.*] Refinement's a thing of the past! ... Manners are *dead*!').[8] Critical approval of Laughton's performance was almost unanimous. *Film Weekly* observed that 'Laughton's acting is a triumph of personality'. John Gamme's review in the same magazine noted: 'This Henry VIII, played with tremendous gusto by Charles Laughton, is a Rabelasian monarch whose connubial adventures and robust buffoonery

entirely liquidate the dryness of an historical character.' With the benefit
of hindsight, Simon Callow concludes that 'it remains one of the greatest
things he [Laughton] did, and one of the most achieved performances
in film history'.[9]

It was, however, the film's financial returns that excited the industry
at the time, and prompted a feverish effort to cash in on its success. Five
hundred extra copies of the print had to be run off at short notice to cope
with the demand for showings, and a sequel, *The Field of Cloth of Gold*
(in which it was intended Laughton would reprise his royal role), was
quickly floated by Korda, but never made. As the film historian Sue
Harper notes, there were a number of other Henrician spin-offs. A West
End show with a Tudor subject, Clifford Bax's *The Rose without a Thorn*
(with Frank Vosper playing Henry), enjoyed a successful revival, and a
number of books on the King and an edition of his letters (dedicated to
Laughton by the editor) were produced to satisfy the public demand for
Henriciana. The script of *Henry VIII* itself was published, the first time
that a feature film had enjoyed this distinction, while newspapers offered
their readers tips on 'How to eat à la Charles Laughton', and marital
advice based on Henry's own turbulent history. Allusions to Laughton's
performance became a stock element in the acts of comics and im-
pressionists across London, and even reached Hollywood, where the
comedian Cliff Edwards added a Henry VIII routine to the musical
review *George White's Scandals*. Finally, the ultimate accolade: a rival
studio made a low-budget parody, set in a public bar: *The Public Life of
Henry the Ninth* (MGM/Ealing, 1935), written and directed by Bernard
Mainwaring, and featuring, among others, the Cockney comedian Wally
Patch, who had a small role in Korda's *Henry VIII* as the King's carver.[10]

Much of the early newspaper coverage was the result of Korda's
shrewd publicity. The pressbooks provided stories concerning every
conceivable aspect of *Henry VIII*, from Laughton's parents' early ambitions that he join the Royal Navy to potted histories of Henry's reign
angled to publicise aspects of the film. Cinema managers were offered,
in addition to the usual publicity posters and foyer cards with their eye-
catching tag-lines (for the customer in search of a sexual thrill: 'What
a King! What a Lover! What a Man!'; or for the more comically inclined:
'He gave his wives a pain in the neck!'), helpful tips on how to stimulate
advance interest in the film – including the suggestion that they erect
castles in their foyers, or hold eating contests ('sponsored by a local
restaurant') in the Laughton style, in which chickens would be consumed
without knife or fork. Korda's mastery of the publicity machinery, and

his uncanny ability to find an angle to spin a story to any audience or
address any situation, were truly ahead of their time. His head of
publicity at London Films, John Myers, was to call him 'a creative genius
in the field' – a result, perhaps, as Kulik suggests, of his early journalistic
training in Hungary.[11]

The huge success of *Henry VIII* almost single-handedly launched the
British film industry as an international concern, and set the agenda for
a number of high-profile historical, or 'costume', films that followed
during the 1930s, including Korda's own *The Rise of Catherine the Great*,
The Private Life of Don Juan and *The Scarlet Pimpernel* (all produced in
1934). Korda himself became for a time the most important figure in
British cinema, and no longer had to go cap in hand to bankers in search
of finance. On the strength of *Henry VIII*'s success, United Artists
signed a long-term deal with Korda, both the Douglas Fairbankses
(Senior and Junior, the former a shareholder in UA) contracted to appear
in subsequent films, and that bastion of corporate finance the Prudential
Assurance Company became a major investor in London Film Productions, allowing Korda to begin work on the massive Denham studios
complex that was to provide the base for his future operations in England
in the 1930s. In addition, Lajos Biró's reputation as a screenwriter was
significantly enhanced, the international careers of Merle Oberon (who
played Anne Boleyn) and Robert Donat (Thomas Culpeper) were
launched, and Charles Laughton's status as a major box-office draw
(rather than simply a superlative character actor) was well and truly
established. Before *Henry VIII*, *Film Weekly* observed, Laughton was
merely a star, after it he was an icon. Merle Oberon (in her Anne Boleyn
costume) made the cover of *Film Weekly* on 16 February 1934, and she
and her fellow 'queens' were suddenly in great demand for product
endorsements and other advertising work. ('Lovely Merle Oberon
chooses Potter and Moore's Powder Cream'; '"Shredded Wheat: I find
it always an interesting dish," says Miss Wendy Barrie' [Jane Seymour];
while Binnie Barnes [Catherine Howard] could be found praising Row-
lands' Macassar Oil in *Film Weekly*.)[12] But the most obvious beneficiary
of the film's success was Korda himself. A man who had left Hollywood
as a failure only three years earlier was now, in the words of the critic
C. A. Lejeune, 'the biggest individual power in European films'. He
had, reputedly, only to pick up the phone in the small hours in London,
and Louis B. Mayer or Samuel Goldwyn would get up from their dinner
to take his call. It was, Korda remarked, 'like having won the Derby
with an unknown horse'.[13]

The boom in British pictures prompted by *Henry VIII*, and the spectacular rise in Korda's own fortunes, were to prove short-lived, however. After the *annus mirabilis* of 1934, when everything he touched seemed to turn to gold, there followed a period of hectic over-investment in projects which either never materialised or failed to produce the profits expected by their investors. The combination of factors that had made the American market temporarily so receptive to British-made films quickly passed, and profits fell as the window in the market contracted. Denham studios, built on a hugely ambitious scale, haemorrhaged the Prudential's money at an alarming rate; expensive projects, such as the lavish *Rembrandt* (1936) and the epic version of Robert Graves's *I, Claudius* (directed, so far as it went, by Josef von Sternberg, 1937), both with Laughton in the title role, either failed to find box-office success or, like the latter, never got beyond the first weeks of shooting. Eventually, in 1937–38, bust followed boom, and the entire British film industry fell into dramatic recession, with numerous smaller producers filing for bankruptcy, and many a corporate investor left angrily blowing on burnt fingers.

Korda, despite having eventually to sell Denham, sailed on with his habitual public air of optimism, floating ambitious new projects, seeing golden rewards over every horizon. But the collapse left a sour taste in the mouths of many of his former backers. Memos circulated within the London financial houses describing him as a plausible rogue, 'a dangerous man with whom to deal', even 'a crook ... and an evil man'.[14] It may be that, as Sarah Street (who has done most to untangle Korda's involvement in the financial dealing that finally hamstrung the industry) has claimed, *Henry VIII* aroused unreasonably optimistic expectations of the profits to be made by British films in America. Korda's example may have 'opened the floodgates of city money to irresponsible producers' and, in the long term, his 'profligacy influenced the city's negative attitude ... probably more than any other British company'.[15] But Korda can hardly be blamed for the greed of those who jumped on the British film bandwagon that began to roll after his initial successes. That Korda was persuasive is hardly a crime, especially in the film production business, and that he was profligate in the conception and the funding of both his own and others' ideas is again not something for which he should be castigated. As C. A. Lejeune observed, with a hint of prophecy in 1936, 'he has so many schemes and ambitions that only half of them are able to fructify; but those that do yield a harvest of prestige and profit beyond the average producer's dreams'. Lejeune's estimate of a 50 per cent success rate may have erred on the side of generosity, but her principle was surely a sound one.[16]

ALEXANDER KORDA (1893–1956)

Alexander Korda was born Sándor László Kellner on the outskirts of Túkeve, Hungary on 16 September 1893, the oldest of three brothers. His siblings, Zoltan (b. 1895) and Vincent (b. 1897), were both, as we shall see, to follow him into film-making and join London Films. He took his adopted name, Korda, from the Latin tag 'Sursum Corda' ('lift up your hearts') when he assumed a journalistic pen-name in Budapest during his teens.[17] It was while working as a cub-reporter for a Budapest newspaper that he first met and interviewed Lajos Biró, the playwright who was to become his collaborator, life-long friend and mentor (it was Biró who was subsequently to pave his way into film-making in both Vienna and Hollywood). It was also through journalism that he became involved in the fledgling Hungarian cinema industry. Having been fascinated by the power and potential of the new medium, he founded a number of cinema magazines, including Hungary's first, Pesti Mozi ('Budapest Cinema'), and Mozihét ('Ciné-Weekly'), and used the influence that his roles as editor and principal reviewer brought with them to start making films himself, the first being, allegedly, a highly ambitious-sounding 'short' based upon 'the Freudian theory of dreams'. Korda worked his way up in the hierarchy of Hungarian producers and directors to the point where he was able to form his own company, Corvin Films, and became Commissioner for Film Production in the liberal government of Count Mihály Karoly in the autumn of 1918. But in November 1919 Korda fled Budapest for Vienna with his first wife, the actress Maria Corda (née Farkas), when, in another violent shift in domestic politics, Admiral Horthy's right-wing government ousted the short-lived communist regime of Béla Kuhn (in which Korda, along with Biró, had briefly served as a member of the Directory for the Arts) and Jews and liberals became prime targets for persecution.

In Vienna Korda took up an offer to direct for Sascha Films, a company owned by Count Alexander Kolowrat-Krokowsky, an intermittent contributor to Mozihét. After a couple of successes, he branched out on his own again, but, in what was to become a signature gesture, over-invested massively in an epic production, Samson und Delila (1920), and found himself broke and out of favour with potential creditors. The only recourse was to move on once more, and, after a brief and successful period in Berlin, Korda and Maria moved to Hollywood in 1926 to work for the First National film company. It was in America, paradoxically, that he began to gather around him the nucleus of the European production team which was to stay with him for the rest of his career (including Zoltan Korda, who came to America as an editor, and Biró, who was to produce the scenarios for *Henry VIII* and all Korda's major films in the 1930s, and who was already in Hollywood, working as a scriptwriter and talking up Korda's reputation as a director among the studio bosses).

Korda's career in Hollywood did not last long, however. After a falling-out with the studios over artistic control and the break-up of his marriage to Maria, Korda left for Europe once more and, after a short stay back in Berlin in 1930, and a brief and successful period working for Paramount in Paris (where he made *Marius* [Paramount, 1931], based upon the Marcel Pagnol stage-play), he arrived in London in November 1931. There he was employed to make 'quota' films (the generally low-cost and low-quality films made by American companies through British subsidiaries or agents to meet the demands of the 1927 Cinematograph Films Act) for Paramount's British subsidiary.[18] In February 1932 he, in collaboration with his brothers Zoltan and Vincent and a number of co-investors, including George Grossmith Senior, formed London Film Productions, for whom he immediately contracted Biró and the English playwright Arthur Wimperis as screenwriters. Vincent Korda, who was by training and inclination a painter, had been co-opted, somewhat unwillingly, into the motion-picture business as set-designer for *Marius*. He was to be artistic director for most of Korda's more successful films thereafter. Zoltan joined the company as a director and was to make a number of London Films' most memorable 'empire' features, including *Sanders of the River* (1935), *Elephant Boy* (co-directed with Robert Flaherty, 1937), *The Drum* (1938) and *The Four Feathers* (1939).[19]

A distribution deal was negotiated for London Films' independent productions with United Artists. The latter were currently anxious to acquire good-quality British films to distribute in an American market temporarily in the doldrums owing to the combined debilitating effects of the Depression, the massive expenditure required to re-equip studios for sound, and a costly battle between the majors for control of the key cinema chains. With the majors momentarily over-extended, United Artists saw that the moment was ripe for the successful reception of good independent British films in the lucrative North American market. All that was needed was to find the right project; a film that would convince America that there was more to British movies than cheap, low-quality, 'quota' productions suitable only for domestic consumption. Korda had convinced United Artists' London agent, Richard Norton, that he could find such a film. Now he had to deliver on that promise.

TWO
The Making of *The Private Life of Henry VIII*

Korda enjoyed telling the story that it was hearing a London cabby singing the Harry Champion music-hall song, 'I'm 'Enery the Eighth, I am' in 1931 that gave him the idea for the film. The comic song, of course, has little to do with the King, but memorably records the sentiments of a Londoner, reflecting, with seemingly ill-grounded self-confidence, upon his recent marriage to a neighbour:

> I'm 'Enery the Eighth, I am.
> 'Enery the Eighth, I am, I am.
> I got married to the widder next door;
> She's been married seven times before.
> And every one was an 'Enery;
> She wouldn't 'ave a Willie or a Sam.
> I'm 'er eighth old man, I'm 'Enery;
> 'Enery the Eighth I am.

Before he heard the song, Korda claimed, he had never heard of Henry VIII. But this was a conscious piece of myth-making. He had already, while in Vienna, directed a treatment of Mark Twain's *The Prince and the Pauper* (released in German as *Seine Majestät das Bettelkind* – 'His Majesty the Beggar-child' – [Sascha Films, 1920]), in which Henry has a prominent role. An alternative story credited Lawrence Howard, Charles Laughton's agent, as the inspiration for the choice of Henry as a subject, he having noted the resemblance between the actor and a bust of the King in Korda's suite in the Dorchester.[1] But the real reasons behind the choice of subject for what was, by British standards at least, a big-budget film, probably had (as Korda's nephew Michael has suggested) more to do with prosaic questions of potential income and artists' availability than with chance encounters in taxis. The success of the earlier Twain project, which was also scripted by Biró, and starred

Alfred Schreiber as Henry, was obviously an important stimulus. The film had been shown in Britain in 1927 and received favourable reviews both for its cinematography and for Schreiber's performance. This, coupled with the recent success of a biography of Henry published in 1929 by Francis Hackett, may have indicated to Korda the likely receptiveness of English audiences for a film about the King.[2]

Perhaps more tellingly still, Laughton, with whom Korda wanted to work, had already, at the time of his discussions with the director, been approached to take the lead role in Shakespeare's *Henry VIII* later in the year, as part of Tyrone Guthrie's first season as director of the Old Vic theatre in London.[3] So Laughton's mind might well have already been turning to thoughts of Henry when Korda came to explore possible film roles with him. The actor's own account of the genesis of the idea, given in an interview in February 1935, supports this explanation of events. 'I met Korda in Paris one day', he recalled, 'and we dined and talked about my season at the Old Vic. From this dinner there emerged an audacious plan, that of producing a costume picture based on the life of Henry VIII.'[4]

There were also clear precursors for the sort of film Korda was considering, both in terms of subject matter and approach. In the wake of the great Italian epics such as Enrico Guazzoni's *Quo Vadis?* (Cines, 1913) and Giovanni Pastrone's *Cabiria* (Film Italia, 1914) historical films had become more 'humanised', focusing on the emotional and personal lives of their protagonists, as was the case in Ernst Lubitsch's magnificent *Anna Boleyn* (Ufa, 1920), starring the great German actor Emil Jannings as Henry and Henny Porten as Anne. This was also the mode of Korda's own early foray into the genre, *The Private Life of Helen of Troy*, made in Hollywood for First National in 1927. There was also the precedent of the 1911 silent treatment of Shakespeare's *Henry VIII*, produced and directed by Will Barker, in which Sir Herbert Beerbohm Tree had reprised his stage triumph in the role, to suggest that the theme could find an audience within and beyond the British Isles.[5]

There may equally have been other, less obvious reasons why Henry's life so appealed to Korda. Michael Korda implies a rather misogynistic sub-text to his choice: 'There was something about Henry VIII that appealed to him. On the one hand he was amused by the paradox of Henry's being henpecked by his wives like any ordinary husband; on the other he admired the King's ability to rid himself of the problems by ordering a beheading.'[6] Perhaps, as his nephew suggests, Korda's interest in this theme was prompted by his ongoing marital difficulties during the late 1920s with his soon to be ex-wife, Maria Corda (who boasted to journalists 'in the home, I am the Director' and would reputedly end arguments by breaking his cigars in half). Certainly a director who would cast his wife as Delilah, Helen of Troy, and the flirtatious wife of *Der Tänzer Meiner Frau* ('My Wife the Dancer', Felsom/Ufa, 1925, released in Britain as *Dancing Mad* in 1928), problematic spouses all, would suggest fruitful material for marital psychologists.[7] Whatever the inspiration, having decided upon the project, Korda assembled his team of designers and technicians to begin the work of realising the vision. Vincent Korda was given the role of designer, and Georges Périnal, who had shot Korda's *The Girl from Maxim's* for London Films in Paris in 1932, was brought over as director of photography. Together they were given a shoestring budget and told to produce a convincing representation of Tudor England.

Given the small budget and the limited shooting time it could finance, the film was made as cheaply as possible. Unlike the Italian epics, there could be no vast crowd scenes – even the executions were arranged to *suggest* large crowds rather than show their full extent – and no sumptuous masonry. Vincent Korda built many of the sets overnight, some, it is claimed, for as little as £10 or £12, and certainly many for under £50, even reusing the nails in order to save money. And, once built, they were frequently shot from alternative angles and reused for other scenes, thus maximising their utility. Laughton was later to recall that 'during the making of the film we were often apprehensive that while we were saying our lines the sets would collapse and smother us'.[8] Pieces of antique furniture, borrowed from museums and private collections, and drawn from an alarmingly wide range of historical periods, were deployed artfully on the sets, giving the impression of a well-stocked palace. And Périnal's camera positioning and clever use of shadow and soft focus transmuted the dross of lath and plaster into settings that the critics and audiences alike took for authentic Tudor splendour. Typical of a Korda production, however, the shooting was not without its element of authentic extravagance and showmanship. The food for the banquet scenes was, apparently, prepared at the Savoy Hotel and sent up fresh to the studios for every session (this, at least, was what Korda told the press). Whatever the truth, the critics were convinced, frequently citing the 'lavish' sets as an important part of the film's appeal.[9]

Publicity for *Henry VIII*, however, focused, perhaps wisely, not on the grandeur of the Henrician court but on 'the enigma of Henry's personality', the 'private life' rather than the public role, and stressed,

1. *Korda on location: the garden scene.*

somewhat elliptically, that the plot was 'concerned with the romantic, rather than the historic phase of Henry's reign' (a veiled admission that it would avoid entirely any of the wider political, religious or social issues of the period).[10]

THE PRIVATE LIFE OF HENRY VIII

Starting on the day of Anne Boleyn's execution, and cutting between events in her chambers, the erection of the scaffold and the preparation for Henry's marriage to Jane Seymour, the film rarely ranges beyond the confines of the royal palace or the King's immediate entourage. The emotional resonances created are generally not particularly troublesome either. A degree of ironic detachment from events is encouraged, even when the pathos of Anne's situation is acknowledged and exploited ('THIRD LADY: Anne Boleyn dies this morning. Jane Seymour takes her place tonight! What luck. / FOURTH LADY: For which of them (I wonder)?'), and the dominant mood is one of excitement, reflected in the expectant bustle of the ladies-in-waiting who must replace the 'A' on all the royal bed-linen with 'J', and Jane's own breathless preparations for her wedding ('Now which shall it be – the pearl chaplet or the velvet coif?'). The viewer is invited to sample a range of emotions, but not to linger on any one of them for long, allowing the momentum of the opening sequence to carry them from each event to the next. Cues are offered by the married couple who appear as a surrogate audience at various points in the film, drawn to the execution by the sense of occasion rather than by any more profound motives.

> WIFE (*with deep feeling*): Poor Anne Boleyn! I feel so sorry for her!
> *She bends over the woman in front of her.*
> Would you mind taking off your hat, madam – we can't see the block ... [11]

From the royal wedding, the narrative cuts rapidly ahead to the birth of Prince Edward and reports of Jane's death, an event which leads into the second sequence of parallel plot-lines, those involving Catherine Howard and Anne of Cleves. While the former sets her sights on the crown, the latter is shown wondering how to avoid it, having been picked out for a political marriage to Henry against her will. Again, matched scenes and contrasting emotions structure the narrative, with Catherine arguing with her suitor Culpeper (Robert Donat) for the supremacy of ambition over love ('And if you got your crown, what would it be worth without love?' / 'Love is not all the world, Tom.' / 'It is – or it is nothing!'), while Anne convinces her suitor, Peynell (John Loder) that love can, with a little ingenuity, win out over the demands of politics ('How like a man – to be dead before he is killed! There is always a way out!'). Scenes illustrating Henry's gradual captivation by Catherine – he listens to her singing, and makes clandestine visits to her bedchamber – are intercut with those depicting the public preparations for the Cleves marriage, until the film reaches its comic climax in the sequence on the wedding night, when Henry and Anne, each repelled by the other's appearance and manners, agree an immediate divorce settlement over a game of cards.

From this point onwards the film moves into somewhat more sombre emotional territory, depicting Henry's marriage to Catherine Howard. As the scene-setting caption suggests, all goes well at first ('Catherine was happy with her crown, Henry was happy with his Catherine'). The queen sublimates those of her sexual and emotional energies which cannot focus satisfactorily on Henry (now depicted in middle age, greying at the temples and beginning, despite his efforts, to stoop) into other activities – wagering with feverish excitement on cock-fights and wrestling. But eventually her frustrations and unhappiness lead her to resume her relationship with Culpeper. After a good deal of anguished soul-search-ing, and some close calls with the King in the queen's bedchamber, the affair is discovered, and the inevitable consequence is another public execution – followed, after a cut to Henry in old age, by another marriage, this time to the woman who will be a surrogate mother both for the royal children and for Henry himself, Catherine Parr (Everley Gregg). The latter is first encountered symbolically wiping the nose of the young Prince Edward, and last seen tucking a blanket around Henry's legs as he sits by the fire. In the final shots, the King, his appetites reduced to a pathetic nibble on a chicken leg ('You know you can't digest it,' warns the queen), is shown reflecting on his life with morbid resignation: 'Six wives, and the best of them's the worst!'[12]

In technical terms, *Henry VIII* is, at first glance, somewhat limited in its ambitions, giving rise to the suggestion that it is an *important* film rather than a really great one.[13] Yet, beneath its surface simplicity there is a satisfying complexity to both its sub-texts and its characterisations. Formally, it is highly episodic, suggesting the kind of baldly chrono-logical arrangement of events favoured by the late medieval chronicles, but also foreshadowing in its pacing and quick-cuts across considerable periods of time the kind of comic *grand guignol* effects of the later *Carry On* and *Confessions* films of the 1970s. Thus wife follows wife, and the next marriage follows swiftly on the last divorce or execution in a rapid succession of scenes. Consequently, the film is, as Michael Korda has observed, far 'quicker' than other costume films of the time, a fact that may have recommended it to audiences.[14] Despite the limited amount of screen time spent on establishing either a comprehensive narrative or a credible social context for events, there is none the less a strong sense of coherence to the film, based in part at least (as we shall see) on its careful deployment of familiar motifs from contemporary (1930s) cul-tural and political history to orientate the spectator.

Cinematically, too, the film is artful without ever seeking to dazzle with its technique. Given the technical limitations of the period, Georges Périnal's camerawork and lighting produce impressive effects, evoca-tively suggesting the flickering, torch-lit interior of the great hall in the banquet scenes (most notably in the wrestling sequence, in which the fighters' silhouettes are thrown against the far wall, as if by the light of a fire burning behind the camera – effects that Stanley Kubrick would need the aid of NASA camera technology to better in the interior scenes of *Barry Lyndon* [Warner Brothers, 1975]), as well as the brighter, sunlit interiors of the chamber scenes, set in the windowed upper storeys of the palaces. There is even room for the occasional disorienting angled shot, as when Henry's face is viewed reflected in a hand-mirror as he lectures Culpeper on the benefits of marrying a 'stupid' woman (Jane Seymour), or when the court is viewed from above, through the arch of a high-level wall tomb (complete with reclining crusader effigy), as it processes to the chapel royal for the Seymour wedding. (This shot is reprised to still greater effect to pick out Henry, alone and dwarfed by the scale of the seemingly vast hall, as he grieves over Catherine Howard's adultery.) Through such subtly disorienting shots the camera both suggests the claustrophobic qualities of life in Henry's court, and hints, through its disturbed geometry, at the distorted morality that motivates it. The reprising of the chapel shot also effectively reinforces the theme insistently revisited in the dialogue, of the close proximity of life and death, wedding and execution, in the Henrician universe. The King is drawn back to the chapel where the royal marriages were solemnised at precisely the moment when he must contemplate the execution of his beloved Catherine Howard, just as Anne Boleyn had earlier harked back to her own wedding as she prepared for her execution ('just like my wedding day', she muses, as she hears the noise of the crowds gathering to watch the event).

For all its episodic nature, however, *Henry VIII* does have a thematic coherence, centred on the experiences of its protagonist. Running through the cavalcade of marriages, executions and banquets is the story of Henry's own journey from the childlike vitality and impatience with courtly formality of the early sequences (as when he almost breaks into a run dragging Jane Seymour to the chapel, or bellows, 'A boy! a boy!' on hearing news of the birth of Prince Edward) to the world-weary resignation of the old King, whose only bursts of spirit involve throwing off the blanket that Catherine Parr has carefully wrapped around his legs, and scuttling to the table to nibble on the forbidden chicken leg. If on the way he never really develops emotionally, he does at least acquire a degree of political maturity, suggested in the scene in which he warns the infant prince of the cares of kingship ('Smile while you may ... for you'll find the Throne of England no smiling matter') and in his final decision to maintain a policy of armed neutrality in foreign affairs ('In my youth, in Wolsey's time, I would have accepted one [alliance] ... or the other. But what is the use of new territories and wars, wars, wars?').[15] For better or worse, the heart of *Henry VIII* lies in the role of the King himself, so any discussion of the film must begin there.

LAUGHTON'S HENRY

As Michael Eaton has observed, 'no paying guest comes cold to the welcoming glow of any movie'.[16] He was thinking primarily of the generic expectations that all audiences bring to a film, expectations that they find confirmed or confounded or qualified by each new contribution to a tradition. But there are also more pragmatic factors at play in the shaping of an audience's expectations. Paying customers coming to see *Henry VIII* took their seats already primed for the experience in a number of ways, their interest piqued and their desires aroused to varying degrees by the copious publicity material with which London Films had saturated the media, by their knowledge of the director and leading actors' previous work, and by whatever promotional material the cinema itself had chosen to display in its poster windows and foyer space. Most obviously of all, perhaps, they came prepared by their knowledge (however limited) of the historical narrative that the film claimed to be reproducing, of Henry VIII's own personality and his infamous marriages.

Henry VIII is, arguably, England's best-known historical figure, and probably, as the historian Sir Geoffrey Elton once claimed, the only English king identifiable from his silhouette alone. Thanks to the endless reproduction of Hans Holbein's massive, full-length portrait (now lost), originally designed to dominate the privy chamber at Whitehall, and the same artist's surviving head and shoulders portrait of the King, Henry has become an instantly recognisable figure, as familiar in popular culture as he is in history books or the classroom. But he is instantly recognisable in just that one pose (legs wide apart, hands at his belt, the massive padded shoulders adding a monumental quality to the stance, as he stares defiantly out of the frame), and in the one set of clothes immortalised by Holbein. Reproductions of Holbein's portrait have stamped Henry's visual image on the consciousness of subsequent generations in a way that no single royal icon had done before or has done since. Not even his shrewder and much-painted daughter Elizabeth was able to inspire one image that could convey all that is known about her – or all that popular culture wants to know – in a single take as Holbein's Henry does. Hence, when we think of Henry VIII what we see in our mind is always Holbein's Henry, or the versions of it that have been recycled since its creation.

Shakespeare's *Henry VIII*, although not at the popular end of the Royal Shakespeare Company or London's West End repertoires, has enjoyed a decent record of revivals in the past two centuries. Yet,

2. *Henry VII and Henry VIII by Hans Holbein the Younger
(by courtesy of the National Portrait Gallery).*

tellingly, it is among the few plays in the canon never to have been performed commercially in modern dress. Holbein's costume, and Holbein's pose, have been copied time and again to furnish productions, precisely because they are so effective a short-cut to the character that we all think we know, establishing Henry's identity and persona in the split second of his first appearance. And what is true of Shakespeare has also been true of other theatrical, cinematic and televisual treatments of the King, and the many forms of cultural spin-off that the nostalgia industry has generated. As I write these words, I can look up and see variations of the Holbein icon staring back at me from a variety of items sent by ironically-inclined friends since I began working on the King: a quilted tea-cosy (bright yellow) and set of table-mats bearing the royal bust 'after Holbein' (accompanied by six coasters, each depicting one of his queens), all courtesy of the National Portrait Gallery, a set of postcards, a writing pad, a tea-towel, even a 'gift set' of seven individual wrapped mint chocolates (Henry amid his wives again) – the murderous history of the reign made literally palatable in a memento for the discerning customers of 'Past Times'. Henry is everywhere – or at least everywhere that the tendrils of the contemporary heritage industry or its ironic popular echoes can reach. And everywhere he is as Holbein painted him. He would not look right any other way.

Any actor taking on the role of the King must, then, come to terms with the impact and legacy of Holbein's portrait. It challenges, it provokes, and sometimes it inspires (as it did Emil Jannings in Lubitsch's *Anna Boleyn* or Robert Shaw in *A Man for All Seasons* [dir. Fred Zinnemann, Columbia, 1966]). Laughton, characteristically, embraced that challenge with vigour, rising to meet it head on. He voraciously imbibed as much 'authentic' Tudor atmosphere as he could from the resources to hand. Charles Higham talks of the actor's 'massive researches' in preparation for the role; Elsa Lanchester recalled him 'almost dragging Korda from his desk down to Hampton Court to see the architecture and pictures'. He took Vincent Korda there, too, and it is clear that these trips had a significant impact on the visual representation of the King and his court in the film.[17] Vincent produced what he claimed was an exact reproduction of Hampton Court's great hall in the studio for the banquet scenes. The costumes worn by the queens and courtiers were based closely on the surviving portraiture at Hampton Court and Holbein's sketches in the royal collection, and Laughton was to cite the layout of the rooms and architecture of the palace as a major influence on his performance. He told the *Daily Express*:

3. *Laughton: the Holbein pose.*

I cannot quite say how I got my conception of Henry VIII ... I suppose
I must have read a good deal about him, but for the rest I spent a lot of
my time walking around the old Tudor Palace at Hampton Court, getting
my mind accustomed to the square, squat architecture of the rooms, and
the cloisters. I think it was from the architecture of the houses and the
rooms that I got my idea of Henry.[18]

It was the Holbein portraits that held the principal fascination for Laughton. He visited the National Portrait Gallery on numerous occasions, returning frequently to the surviving cartoon (of Holbein's privy chamber mural, only the life-sized sketch used to transfer the initial drawing to the wall remains to give a sense of the impact of the original). Higham describes how Laughton was 'particularly drawn' to it, and 'grew his beard to precisely the length indicated by Holbein', 'combed his hair meticulously' to match what could be seen of the King's coiffure under his bonnet, and tried to turn the image from a two-dimensional portrait into a living character. Critics were almost unanimous in their approval of the actor's success. 'He sometimes looks as if he had stepped from the frame of Holbein's painting,' observed the *New York Times* reviewer.[19]

Elsa Lanchester's account of the rehearsal process charts the painstaking efforts taken to realise the role: 'gradually the character began to soak in. One day he would think he had got the walk, the next day he would lose it; then he would get a look in the eye and let that stew for a few days. After a week's shooting on the picture, I should say he found himself getting into the part.'[20]

The achieved effect is indeed striking. At his first appearance, framed by a stone doorway and backed by a fleur-de-lys hanging, Laughton is Holbein's image personified. But, having held the pose for a second, he strides into the room. The portrait is made massive, imposing, flesh, but with a hint of mischievous humour in the eyes and angle of the shoulders that humanises it. Frequently, when he is not in motion, Laughton will fall back into the pose, legs apart, the angle of the head held just as Holbein has it, whether to remind the audience of his historical role, or to 'find' the part again himself (as Callow and Lanchester both suggest, Laughton needed to fix a role physically if he was to sustain his characteristically intense level of performance, and so would rely on a certain tic, trait or, as here, stance to give him the necessary bodily orientation to generate the performance). Laughton even tries, less successfully, to walk in the same posture, producing an awkward goosestep, but such moments are mercifully rare.

Other Tudor portraits studied during those research trips to the galleries were probably also important stimuli. As Callow has observed, the ageing of the King is managed splendidly in the course of the film, both by the subtle variations of the make-up (a touch of grey here, a hint of white at the jowls and forehead, the shaving of his eyebrows) and by subtle changes in the actor's posture. The final image of the old King

4. *Henry VIII by an unknown engraver (by courtesy of the National Portrait Gallery).*

5. *The King in old age.*

seems to have been based upon a number of engravings of the aged
Henry by unknown artists that convey precisely the sagging facial
muscles and prim pose of the hands that Laughton adopts for his final
speech to camera. Lanchester, too, is said to have based her make-up and
wig on 'a small oval cameo of Anne in the National Portrait Gallery',
and her fellow queens were dressed as closely as possible to the surviving
portraits of the originals.[21]

One further portrait may well also have had a role to play. One of the
most striking shots in the film is that in which Laughton, staring intently
out of a leaded window, impatiently drums his fingers on the pane,
awaiting the signal that Anne Boleyn has been put to death. The camera
first picks out, in close shot, a hand tapping against the leaded glass in
time with the hammers of the workmen constructing the scaffold, then
pans right to the King's face, disturbingly close-up at the next pane, and
holds that shot, before fading back to a view of the scaffold. It is an
unnerving sequence, combining real menace with the kind of quizzical
intensity in the King's expression that is characteristic of Laughton's
performance. And it is also uncannily like the image of a laughing child
(or perhaps he is a court fool) staring from a leaded window in the
painting known as *Boy looking through a casement*, currently on display

6. *Boy looking through a casement (The Royal Collection © 2002, Her Majesty Queen Elizabeth II).*

in the Renaissance Gallery at Hampton Court, which conveys a similar mixture of the arresting and the disturbing in the subject's expression. The image, described in the catalogue of royal paintings at Hampton Court in 1529 as 'Full face, the head and shoulders of a youth in black cap and tunic looking through a leaded casement, his right hand tapping the glass' may well have been the source of the cinematic image, providing further evidence of the extent of Laughton and Korda's researches, and their influence on the finished film.[22]

Another more substantial influence on the actor was almost certainly

Jannings's performance in Lubitsch's *Anna Boleyn*. The German star
gave the role a number of the distinctive touches that would also characterise Laughton's Henry. He ate boisterously (although Laughton
greatly exaggerated the trait to comic effect), brought a powerful
physicality to his Holbeinesque poses, and played the role with a broad,
childlike emotional palette similar to that Laughton would deploy. Jannings's Henry was, however, a more brutal figure than Laughton's,
rougher cast in his sexuality, and bringing a distinct physical danger to
those scenes in which he pursued his potential 'conquests'. Despite his
childlike simplicity, Henry, in Jannings's portrayal, was a king who would
not, one suspected, flinch at rape, should his target prove resistant to his
ham-fisted advances. Laughton's Henry, by contrast, was a more refined
creation, more complex and ironic in its tones. Hindsight, indeed, imparts
a distinctly camp quality to the coy, overtly 'constructed' quality of
Laughton's pose as the great womaniser, especially in those scenes in
which he plays up his reluctance to be prodded into another marriage by
his counsellors ('Marry again – breed more sons? Coarse brutes! ... Am
I the King or a breeding bull?').[23] Laughton the gay actor (although he
probably never fully came to terms with his own sexuality), playing a
Bluebeard monarch posing as a coy celibate, gives the role an extra
richness and resonance for modern audiences, suggesting what Steven
Cohan has termed 'queer tensions' that neither Laughton nor Korda
could have foreseen.[24] This campness was almost certainly not what
Laughton himself wished to convey. As Michael Korda has suggested,
the actor's sensibilities about his own public persona, and his desire to
project a marketable heterosexual image were probably the principal
motives that drew him to 'the majestically masculine role of Henry
VIII' in the first place.[25] The performance that he and Korda were to
craft was, however, anything but simplistically magnificent in its masculinity. As Chapter 5 will suggest, Laughton, in his search for a means of
negotiating Henry's relationships with his wives, seems to have found
his inspiration in the role's childlike qualities – a performance choice
that only added to the role's ambiguities and depth of interest.

THREE
Korda, Englishness and
the 'International Film'

Early press coverage of London Films was fascinated by the flamboyance and cosmopolitanism of the Korda organisation. A *Film Weekly* feature, published in August 1933, observed that 'eight languages are spoken among [Korda's] staff ... He will break off a conversation in English to answer the telephone in Italian, and the next time it rings he will be replying to questions in German.' Stephen Watts, recycling the same story, claimed that the London Films offices 'might well be subtitled "International House"'. So 'foreign', indeed, did Korda's new studio at Denham seem, that Douglas Fairbanks Jnr allegedly suggested that it needed a British Consulate to cater for its few native employees. And what was true of London Films in general applied also to *Henry VIII* in particular. It is often pointed out that the most famous 'British' film of the time was actually produced by a nucleus of three Hungarians (Alexander and Vincent Korda, and Biró), a French cameraman (Périnal), and an American supervising editor (Harold Young).[1]

Such ironies were not lost on Korda himself, who was not averse to disarming a potentially difficult situation with a joke. When his naturalisation documents arrived at Denham in 1936, for example, he celebrated with his workers on the set of his current costume drama, *Rembrandt*. His first words as a British citizen were a cheery, 'to hell with the bloody foreigners!'[2] But such light-hearted comments should not detract from the seriousness of the issues at stake. The fact that legislation such as the 1927 Cinematographic Films Act (see the next section for the details) had led not to a resurgence of a home-grown British cinema but the import of artists and cinematographers from abroad, was not greeted with universal acclaim. Resentment of immigration into Britain in general in the 1930s found a point of particular purchase in attacks upon the film industry. If both Britain's national image abroad and the morale of its own citizens at home were as reliant upon the domestic film industry as the government claimed, what damage was being done by the alleged dominance of that industry by foreigners, especially Jewish émigrés from Central and Eastern Europe, with no sense of, or obvious stake in, 'the national heritage'? Such sentiments underlay a range of public statements ranging from the overtly racist polemics of political extremists to the supercilious responses of establishment cinema critics and intellectuals. Lieutenant-Colonel A. H. Lane's diatribe, *The Alien Menace* (reprinted in a third edition in 1932), launched a vitriolic attack on what the author termed 'the German-American alien' (read 'Jewish') control of film distribution in Britain; a conspiracy aimed at 'destroying our patriotism, our traditions, and our ideals'. Lane's preferred solution was a ban on all 'subversive films' (a category in which he included American gangster movies as well as the 'Moscow propaganda' of Sergei Eisenstein). More subtly, Graham Greene, writing in *The Spectator*, acidly observed:

> England, of course, has always been the home of the exiled, but one may express a wish that émigrés would set up trades in which their ignorance of our language and culture was less of a handicap; it would not grieve me to see Mr Alexander Korda seated before a cottage loom in some eastern county, following an older and better tradition.[3]

World Film News was to repeat the same point in a heavily ironic attack on the immigrant film producers in September 1937:

> on these gentlemen and their creative attitude to our English industries, our countryside, our people (and our banking system) we depend for the projection of our national life. On their deep, inborn sense of our history, our heritage, and our customs we depend for the dramatization of our English traditions as well as for the more mundane business of fulfilling our British quota.[4]

The issue was exacerbated at the time that *Henry VIII* was being shot by the influx of German artists and technicians fleeing from the newly established Nazi regime. And the trades unions (the Association of Cinematograph Technicians in particular) and elements of the right-wing media were both very vocal at this time in opposing the newcomers; again, Jewish émigrés were singled out for especially venomous attention (one journalistic diatribe against the influx deplored 'the prostitution of [the film industry] by sex-mad and cynical financiers ... mainly Jewish'). A more positive spin was put on the issue by *Film Weekly*, whose 1934 'British Film Special Number' began with an editorial discussing the 'one important difference' between this and previous 'British Specials': the presence of so many 'international' names among the schedule of domestic producers and artists:

> A list of names picked from it at random reads like a roll of delegates to a screen league of nations. You may wonder, as you turn the pages, if British films are really 'British' any more. In a sense they are not. The parochial atmosphere has been stamped out of them. The proportion of 'foreign' talent employed in the production of the average 'English' film has increased to a point undreamed of a year or two ago. Stern patriots and political isolationists may deplore the change. For our part, we welcome it ... The cosmopolitan composition of the outstanding productions of 1933–34 has carried them to success in America, France, and many other countries besides our own. The result? Busy studios. More employment. More money available for the provision of still better entertainment.[5]

The debate was aired in Parliament on a number of occasions. In November 1937, for example, R. C. Morrison, the Labour MP for North Tottenham, observed in the House of Commons: 'there is a good deal of humbug talked about British films ... In 1933 British films were put on the map of America by a Hungarian who produced the film called *The Private Life of Henry VIII*. If you look through the list of British films, you will have some difficulty in discovering a British point of view.'

It was all very well contemporaries calling for the 'projection' of British – or more accurately English – values by the cinema industry, but it was clearly important which version of those values would be projected. As Sarah Street has suggested, there were a number of competing versions of Englishness on offer to cinema-goers in the 1930s, and some struck contemporaries as more English than others.[6]

THE PROJECTION OF BRITAIN: CINEMA AND NATIONAL IDENTITY

By the turn of the twentieth century, Britain, and more particularly England, was in search of a new sense of national identity.[7] Those things that had once made Britain distinctive (and distinctively 'Great') – a long and largely unbroken monarchical tradition, a powerful navy, a well-developed heavy industrial base and a worldwide empire – were no longer a uniquely British preserve. By the late 1920s officials in the

Foreign Office and Department of Overseas Trade were clearly aware
that there was a heated peacetime propaganda war being fought on a
global scale and that Britain was losing it by default. Hence there began
a conscious search for new values, and a new cultural identity which
could be fostered both at home and abroad to further Britain's economic
fortunes and counter the propaganda industries of not only the totali-
tarian states, Russia, Italy and especially Germany, but also former allies
such as France and the USA. But how a peacetime propaganda campaign
should be organised was a vexed question. The kind of assertive methods
employed during wartime were felt to be inappropriate to the new
conditions of peace, and such 'bragging' was, in any case, thought to be
essentially un-English by many of those responsible for the new in-
itiative.[8]

Sir Stephen Tallents (a former diplomat and secretary to the Empire
Marketing Board who was later to become public relations officer at the
BBC and director general of the Ministry of Information) published a
clarion call in 1932 for what he called 'The Projection of England', a
phrase that was to become synonymous with British propaganda activities in the 1930s. 'No civilized country', he argued, 'can today afford
either to neglect the projection of its national personality, or to resign
its projection to others.' Thus he proposed to develop 'in the borderland
which lies between Government and private enterprise, a school of
national projection'.[9]

The search for a readily exportable national identity found its focus
in a renewed interest in pre-industrial culture, and particularly in the
compelling conjunction of artistic energy, political and religious renewal,
and the roots of imperial expansion identified with the Tudor period.
This had the advantage, as Paul Greenhalgh has argued, of bypassing
the more problematic aspects of Britain's contemporary situation – a
crumbling imperial hegemony, depressed industrial base and increasingly
fraught labour, class and race relations – in favour of an image of a
'purer', prosperous Britain untouched by the ills of modernity, in which
monarch and people were united in an untroubled sense of national
purpose. Thus representations of Shakespeare's Globe Theatre and the
trappings of Tudor monarchy were packaged into a version of 'Olde
Englande' that was Britain's contribution to world fairs from the Paris
Exposition of 1900 to the Texas Centennial in 1936.[10]

Fundamental to this image of 'Olde Englande' was the figure of John
Bull who represented the kind of unassertive, essentially benevolent
persona that the government's developing propaganda arm was intent

upon projecting. As Greenhalgh describes him, the John Bull persona embodied a number of aspects of the newly refashioned British/English identity: 'This comfortable, portly gentleman was at once a shrewd northern mill owner, the Lord Mayor of London, a merry wood-chopper, and Sir Toby Belch; he was relatively uncultured in the highest sense, but he had the type of attitude to life that made him the perfect representative of English bourgeois values.' From the list of qualities described here, it is easy to see how the ostensibly solid, but actually protean and timeless character of 'plain John Bull' was readily conformable to other figures who would (and still do) play a part in the projection of England's heritage, notably Shakespeare's other great portly gourmand, Sir John Falstaff, Dickens's archetypically benevolent bourgeois, Mr Pickwick, and, as we shall see, Korda and Laughton's reinterpretation of Henry VIII.

The crucial role of the film industry (and especially the 'heritage film' industry) in fostering this image of Britain had long been recognised. The view at the Foreign Office was, crudely, that 'Trade follows the film, not the flag' and that 'one foot of film equals a dollar of trade'. As Sue Harper notes, the debates in Parliament prior to the passing of the 1927 Cinematograph Films Act 'marshalled historical film straightforwardly into notions of the national interest'.[11] The then leader of the Labour opposition, Ramsay MacDonald, called explicitly for British filmmakers, acting in the national interest, 'to use our national scenery; to use our history; which is more magnificent for film productions than the history of any other nation in the world'.[12]

The resulting Act was a response to a perceived threat that was both economic and cultural. By 1925, only around 5 per cent of the films shown in British cinemas were British made, and this lack of a distinctly native cinema was perceived to have far-reaching and dangerous consequences. Hollywood had for some years dominated the world market, but in the days of silent films, the cultural impact of this dominance had been limited. With the arrival of sound, the national cultural identity encoded in a film became far more obvious and central to its impact. The predominance of American accents and cultural references in the new 'talkies' gave added impetus to the demands for the development of a domestic cinema industry. As the *Daily Express* was to lament on 18 March 1927, 'we have several million people, mostly women, who, to all intent and purpose, are temporary American citizens'.[13]

In an attempt to address this problem directly, the 1927 Act established a quota of British-made films for renters and distributors, starting with

5 per cent and rising to 20 per cent in 1936.[14] The results were, however, not impressive. Although a number of good-quality films were made in the wake of the Act, its chief effect was to stimulate the production of so-called 'quota quickies' (cheap, low-grade films made in Britain by the American majors through their British subsidiaries, or through contracts with British companies, to satisfy the quota), leaving the US companies free to continue to import high-quality films made in Hollywood at the normal rate. The result was thus a further blow to the reputation of the native industry and its products.

Alongside the attempt to defend Britain against American cultural influence, the government sought to encourage the promotion of suitably British values in those films produced at home, in order to take the propaganda war abroad. Tallents's *The Projection of England*, as its central metaphor suggests, identified a clear role for film (which he saw as exerting an 'incalculable moral and emotional influence') in his wider national and international agenda: 'If a nation would be truly known and understood in the world, it must set itself actively to master and to employ the new, difficult and swiftly developing modes which science has provided for the national personality.'[15]

The idea of a Foreign Office film unit had been floated as early as 1920, but fell through on grounds of cost. Subsequently the emphasis shifted towards encouraging private film-makers to produce and distribute abroad films with a distinctive and positive British cultural content. As well as not being a direct drain on the British taxpayer,[16] such films had the added advantage of appearing less obviously propagandistic in both content and provenance. They were consequently thought more likely to have a favourable reception abroad, especially in those markets like the USA seen to be hostile to overt propagandising (as one journalist noted, 'the self-respecting American is down on all propagandists, as the self-respecting housewife is down on vermin').[17] As a Department of Overseas Trade memorandum noted in 1929: 'pictures with human interest are needed: there must be touches that audiences can appreciate, even though the subjects of films do not appeal from a trade point of view, and the industrial or national propaganda must be kept in the background'.[18]

Domestically, too, new imperatives were driving a politics of 'projection'. In the wake of electoral reforms in 1918 and 1928 a new mass electorate was created, leaving many politicians with a sense that British democracy was entering a new and potentially vulnerable phase. The 1918 Representation of the People Act brought a 300 per cent increase in the number of people eligible to vote, and thus, in the words of Stanley Baldwin, placed the fate of the empire in the hands of 'millions of untrained and inexperienced voters'. Such an 'untrained' electorate, it was feared, might easily vote on grounds of pure self- or class interest, or fall prey to demagogues, and thus needed a careful induction into its role and responsibilities.[19] At a time when visits to British cinemas were running at over 900 million a year, the film industry seemed an obvious means by which that induction could be performed.[20]

With the 1928 Equal Franchise Act, a whole new constituency of young women (the so-called Flapper Vote) was added to this already volatile electorate. Such women, it was felt, were particularly prone to appeals to the emotions and sentiment, and so were especially in need of 'training' and guidance. According to contemporary opinion, such women were also precisely the audience for whom historical films were perceived to hold the strongest and most distinct appeal. Hence the cinema was invested with a new responsibility to produce socially responsible images of traditional British values and characteristics that could be 'projected' to this particular niche domestic audience.

It is in this context that we must read the production of historical films such as *Henry VIII*, and the succession of 'costume pictures' that followed it in the 1930s, films based in that desirable pre-industrial 'golden age', which promoted a strong sense of a British heritage, while also suggesting more subliminally the superiority of British culture and its role in world affairs. Such films fitted ideally the model identified by Tallents for the projection of British history and values. But did they perform their intended role with a sufficient degree of responsibility? In the case of *Henry VIII* opinions differed.

The unimpeachable 'Englishness' of *Henry VIII* seemed self-evident to Ernest Betts, who declared in his introduction to the printed script: 'In *The Private Life of Henry VIII* we have a film of taste, of wit, of good, boisterous humour, as English as a Sussex field.' H. Nobel Hall, the head of the Paris office of the Travel Association, also praised the film, citing the 'enormous success' of a screening in Paris in promoting the kind of image of Britain that he wanted to project abroad. It was also to receive strong approval from the Foreign Office. When, for example, it opened in Peru, billed as 'a United Artists production', civil servants intervened directly with British representatives in Lima to get it credited to London Films, thus making its 'authentically British' origins explicit.[21]

The film was, however, also to provoke considerable opposition from within establishment circles, and for a variety of reasons. Morality and 'taste' loomed large in many of the objections. In the immediate after-math of the première, Lord Cottenham, writing in the *Daily Telegraph*, criticised its portrayal of Henry himself as 'a vulgar travesty of history'. Laughton's king was, he claimed, a 'dissolute buffoon', whose 'revolting habits' represented 'the acme of bad taste'.[22] Beyond provoking such knee-jerk reactions to the King's table manners, the film was also instru-mental, as Sue Harper has shown, in prompting a wider debate about the social utility of historical films, and their role in the 'projection' of England. In 1935 the annual meeting of the Historical Association passed a resolution declaring: 'This meeting … is gravely concerned at the effect on children and adults of films purporting to represent historical personages which are being shown in picture palaces, and considers that steps should be taken to assist teachers and others to estimate the ac-curacy of such films.'[23]

The question of historical authenticity inevitably became tangled up with the issue of the film's role as cultural propaganda. It was all very well to present British monarchs on film in dignified settings – as Herbert Wilcox was to do in his two treatments of Victoria's reign for RKO, *Victoria the Great* (1937) and *Sixty Glorious Years* (1938) – even if the absolute 'accuracy' of such films was questionable, but what of those treatments which, like *Henry VIII*, showed them 'unbuttoned' or even in various states of actual undress? And what were the political con-sequences of offering such 'disrespectful' views of imperial history abroad? In 1934 Sir Frank Saunderson urged the Secretary of State for India, Sir Samuel Hoare, to ban *Henry VIII* outright on the subcontinent, as it was likely to have a 'detrimental effect on the audience'.[24]

On the question of accuracy Korda and his associates were quick to join the debate, and the terms at issue were relatively clear. Charles Laughton defended the historical authenticity of *Henry VIII* in an inter-view with Hubert Cole published in *Film Weekly* in February 1934. He claimed, somewhat misleadingly: 'most of the dialogue was copied straight from contemporary records of Henry's actual words … As a matter of fact the only incident in the whole picture for which we can't quote full historical chapter and verse is the card-playing scene with Anne of Cleves. And even that is surmisable, I think.' Others were not so sure. C. R. Beard, author of 'The Costume and Arms of the Yeoman of the Guard', launched a swingeing attack on the film's historical inaccuracies in an article whose title, 'Why Get It Wrong?', offers a succinct account of its thesis. *Henry VIII*, he claimed, 'may be good entertainment, but it is feeble history, bad psychology, and worse archaeology'. Curiously, Beard commended the film's kitchen scenes as 'all too brief works of art'; but recoiled from the depiction of court life 'above stairs' in horror. Other than Laughton himself, he complained, the actors did not seem to have made any effort to look like the historical figures they were impersonating. The costumes were largely anachronistic, the 'tonsorial eccentricities' of beard, quiff and permanent wave were ridiculously inappropriate, and where, oh where, were the insignia of the Order of the Garter that Thomas Cromwell and his fellow knights of the Order should, by the terms of its statutes, have been wearing at all times?[25]

Still more specific, and potentially more contentious in practical terms, was the question of where, exactly, Korda, Biró and Wimperis had found the historical materials that they claimed to have reproduced in the film. Francis Hackett, the author of a highly successful biography of Henry, thought he knew, and allegedly threatened to sue London Films for plagiarism, claiming that his own work had been used without permission in furnishing the screenplay. Certainly there are some strong similarities between the two narratives in their focus on similar key scenes and details, and in their interpretation of events. On other important matters (most notably the characterisation of Anne of Cleves and Catherine Howard), however, the two treatments are very different. And Korda was characteristically categorical in his response to the accusation. Paul Tabori quotes him as saying 'in all the film there is not one incident, not one line or phrase, borrowed from Mr Hackett. If, by any chance, there are minor similarities – and I am not aware of any – that is because we both borrowed from history.' On the question of where, precisely, that 'history' was located, Korda remained silent (Laughton's airy allusion to 'contemporary records' suggests original research, but the timescale of the project – Biró reputedly produced the first treatment for the screenplay overnight – rules out the prospect of regular treks to the Public Record Office by the writers). Faced with such a vigorous refutation, the threat of litigation was quickly withdrawn.[26]

Invariably, however, defending the accuracy of the film also entailed involvement in the wider question of its cultural impact. In his apologia for *Henry VIII*, Philip Lindsay, the historical novelist contracted to act as its 'technical adviser', argued an extremely ambitious case for what the historical film as a genre could do for the sensibilities of British audiences. It could, he declared, turn back the tide of pictures focusing on 'the shoddy, vulgar, and brutal things of today'. Asserting that 'we need romance terribly today', he predicted:

In future ... we will be shown the great achievements of men in the past; we will see heroic deeds and splendid women ... Costume films, I firmly believe, will bring back a sense of honour and honesty. Instead of lads striving to be Cagneys, they will wish to be d'Artagnans, and the women will expect a certain finesse, a certain beauty about love-making. Costume films will bring colour into life ... Too long have we been taught to despise ourselves ... The films will teach us self-respect.[27]

In presenting the past, then, *Henry VIII* would, in Lindsay's view, not only reflect the present, but also have a powerful influence upon the future. While he remained reticent about Lindsay's more grandiose claims, Korda may have had some sympathies with that suggestion at least, as we shall see. Certainly, Lindsay's sense that an individual's, even a whole society's, sense of identity could be shifted by a determined rethinking and representation of cultural symbols would have rung true to the director's ears.

KORDA AND 'INTERNATIONAL' ENGLISHNESS

Korda was a man for whom the constructedness of social identity was clear from an early point in his career. A minor anecdote from his first days in the Hungarian film industry offers an insight into his later strategies. Talking of his move from newspaper journalism into film production, Korda observed ruefully, 'I earned £60 a month [rather more than he had as a journalist]. But films were considered something rather lowly – more lowly than newspapers.' Typically he negotiated the social degradation involved by making a compensatory change to his public image. 'Cigars were large and cheap at the time. [So] we smoked cigars to show that we were important and to make up for our loss of position.'[28] A simple change of habit, then, could refashion not only his personal image, but that of the entire industry in the public eye. To adopt the lifestyle of the well-to-do and influential was the first step towards joining them. It was a method Korda was to employ frequently in his subsequent enterprises, and which was to be remarked upon by many who knew him or charted his career. The British documentary film-maker Basil Wright spoke of Korda's 'chameleon-like qualities', and C. A. Lejeune was to describe his 'extraordinary skill for acclimatising himself'. But this 'knack' might more accurately be seen as a highly adapted form of the refugee's natural survival instinct – that assimilationist strategy of the diasporic communities that Woody Allen was to burlesque in *Zelig* (Orion/Warner Brothers, 1983). On arriving in Vienna, Lejeune claimed, Korda 'became Viennese overnight'. On coming to England, according to Alan Wood, he 'rapidly mastered, not only the English tradition, but even the English idiom'. Within two years, it was said that, although he spoke 'with a pronounced accent ... his command of English is not merely thorough, it is well above that of the average Englishman'.[29]

That this capacity for rapid, *partial* assimilation (Korda, as he told a number of interviewers, deliberately fostered that slight element of distance – the air of the 'exotic' – that came with a 'broken' English accent) was a carefully constructed career strategy, was evident from the first move that he, then a twenty-six-year-old unemployed director, made, from Budapest to Vienna in 1919. On arrival, Korda immediately, in Kulik's words, 'affected a grandiose lifestyle which he could ill-afford', living in expensive hotels and hiring chauffer-driven cars in an attempt to give the right impression to potential investors. As with that early shift from cigarettes to cigars, Korda was fashioning an image that played to people's preconceptions, here of the movie mogul, of high living, culture and, most of all, success. And, as with the cigars, it seems to have worked every time he tried it. In Vienna it was the Imperial Hotel and the Grand, in Berlin, the Eden, in Paris, the Ritz, and in London it was to be the Savoy and the Dorchester. And everywhere he sought out the most expensive and longest-established tailors, having suits made (usually on credit) in a very traditional cut. In each case the image was the same; an extravagant, but ultimately conservative, *dependable*, opulence, a combination of the glamour of the foreign, coupled with the reliability of 'old money', that covered a fledgling entrepreneur (and one in a fragile, fledgling industry) in a rapidly acquired patina of conventional cultural capital.[30]

Korda was, more generally, always adept at rapidly acquiring the trappings, if not the substance, of a national identity for his operations. He chose an image of Big Ben for the trademark of London Films, thus asserting the Englishness of the products in a way that Sir Stephen Tallents and the men from the Ministry would have heartily approved. But in doing so he was only repeating a formula that had proved successful in his native Hungary, where he had wrapped his first substantial film-making enterprise in the images of national tradition, buying up the name of the Transylvanian film company, Corvin Films, for whom he had previously worked, and using it as the banner for his own new company, while adopting the coat of arms of the Renaissance king

Martinus Corvinus (after whom the company was named) as his personal emblem. Equally formulaic, albeit in a different key, was the way in which London Films bought up a 'stable' of actors on five-year contracts (paying them £20 per week) to provide the basis of a repertory company for their films. Among those hired were four 'starlets', each of whom was typecast for a stereotypical role in future productions: Wendy Barrie and Joan Gardner (the future Mrs Zoltan Korda) were to be the 'typical English girls', Merle Oberon (later the second Mrs Alexander Korda) was the 'exotic woman', and Diana Napier was identified for roles calling for what Korda described as 'the high-class bitch'. Here again Korda was acquiring an off-the-peg collection of conventional cultural signifiers, ready to be deployed in the international film market as instantly recognisable markers of 'authentic' Englishness.

Throughout his career Korda also habitually signed up or attached to his enterprises in less formal ways anyone who he thought might provide an entrée into establishment circles or who might, more importantly, impress likely investors in the City. Thus, famously, at one time he would count among his 'employees' the sons of no fewer than three former or future prime ministers: Oliver (later Lord) Baldwin, the director Anthony Asquith and Randolph Churchill. In addition to adopting that central (and readily identifiable) symbol of Big Ben for his films, Korda set about courting a number of establishment figures – most of them associated with the die-hard wing of the Conservative Party – as associates for London Films and for his social circle. Two Tory politicians, Captain A. C. N. Dixey and William Brownlow (later Lord Lurgan) were invited to join the board as investors in London Films, and Korda quickly made overtures to Winston Churchill, who was added to the team of writers associated with LFP in 1934.[31] That Korda should have sought to identify himself with the die-hard Tories, a group on the right of the party, characterised during the 1920s by its highly chauvinistic stance on foreign affairs and containing a number of distinctly anti-Semitic figures, is another of the ironies that attended his career. It is tempting to dismiss it as a short-term, cynical attempt to wrap London Films in the Union Jack while it established itself as a going concern (and, indeed, within eighteen months both Dixey and Brownlow had disappeared from the board). But, as we shall see in the next chapter, there was a logic to the association above and beyond its capacity to provide Korda's business interests with a further level of distinctly 'English' identity.[32]

What was true of Korda's general career was also reflected in his work as a director, and in the philosophy that underpinned it. It is no surprise that a man whose career took him from Túkeve, through Budapest, Vienna, Berlin, Hollywood and Paris before he finally reached London, favoured (indeed, based his whole approach to film-making on) what he termed the 'international' film. What is perhaps more striking is the degree to which Korda's sense of the 'international' was rooted in a strong sense of indigenous national culture. As he observed in 1933:

> the phrase 'international film' is a little ambiguous. I do not mean that a film must try to suit the psychology and manners of every country in which it is going to be shown. On the contrary, to be really international, a film must first of all be truly and intensely national. It must be true to the matter in it.

As Kulik has observed: 'the international film was to be one which relied on stereotypical situations and characters peculiar to one country, but recognized immediately by audiences of other countries'. With such a situation, as Korda claimed: 'An outsider often makes the best job of a national film. He is not cumbered with an excessively detailed knowledge and associations. He gets a fresh slant on things.'[33] As we shall see, both an 'intensely national' view of English history and Korda's 'fresh slant on things' were to be influential in the production and success of *Henry VIII*.

In *Henry VIII* the politics of 'race' – of identity and belonging – are inflected through the assertion of the contemporaneousness of the past, its familiarity to modern audiences rather than its strangeness. 'If five minutes after the picture has begun the audience is still aware that it is a costume film', Korda was to observe in 1934,

> then it is because it is a bad film ... It is only by making people quickly forget that the theme is the past ... that history can be made [into] cinema entertainment. The two secrets of that are atmosphere and intimacy ... By the need for intimacy I mean the projection of the feeling that the people in the film – despite differences of time and circumstance – are just like you and me.[34]

In *Henry VIII*, the King and his court are presented in precisely this way as 'just like you and me', and so, by implication, 'you and me' might conceivably be just like them. National identity and heritage can be acquired through the conscious adoption of stereotypical traits and features (those cigars again). It is tempting to read Korda's concern with history as spectacle – with the breadth of allusion and the reproduction of a superficial 'gloss' of period flavour rather than the 'depth' of its historical roots – in this same light. 'Our difficulty', he declared, in an interview in May 1938,

> is that you cannot convey a proper sense of the English spirit ... unless you go down to the roots. Roots strike deep into history and may be very local things. In America, where roots are near the surface, they are not easily interested in what lies deep down in other countries, and unless we can interest America there may be no great market for our own films ... I think that we are compelled, as far as world markets are concerned, to stick to stories based on broad issues of the national life ... stories that dig deep into national roots start with a handicap.[35]

It might be that the past is a foreign country, but for Korda, whose sense of the present was always that of an outsider, stressing its familiarity was the more attractive prospect, psychologically as well as financially. His interest in the internationalism of the national, of the ready translatability of all stereotypes between national cultures, was part of a refashioning of the past which was also a refashioning of the self.

Issues of 'race' and nationality, however, in the 1930s had rather more pressing implications than furnishing speculation about the post-modern constructedness and fluidity of personal identity. In putting his ideas into practice, Korda, as we have seen, surrounded himself with an army of artists, technicians and writers who were predominantly émigrés, and frequently Hungarian or German Jewish in origin. It would be doing him a disservice to see this as merely an artistic or commercial strategy. In employing émigré artists and technicians, he was, as Kulik and Kevin Gough-Yates have both suggested, offering a safe haven, even an escape route out of continental Europe, for Jewish intellectuals, film industry specialists and their families who faced the prospect of persecution or worse in their home countries. As Gough-Yates has implied, the contracts that Korda offered to such people were often more philanthropic gestures than serious commercial propositions, but they allowed the recipients to accept charity while, as Kulik notes, retaining their dignity.[36] In this spirit Korda provided the money for Alfred Kerr and his family to travel to Britain by commissioning a script (never to be filmed) concerning the life of Napoleon's mother, while Carl Zuckmayer was given an advance against future scripts, enabling him to move to London from Zurich, where he was living after fleeing from Vienna. A similar degree of philanthropy often motivated Korda's 'investments' in scripts, or potential scripts, from émigrés already in Britain who had fallen on hard times. As Michael Korda suggests, the director's decision to buy the rights to Romola Nijinsky's biography of her husband, and to renew those rights with periodical further payments, probably had as much to do with ensuring that his fellow Hungarians had an income on which to live than with any serious intention to shoot the film. Equally, his offers of contracts to the Hungarian Bauhaus artist Laszlo Moholy Nagy (to produce artwork for *Things to Come* and to direct a short film about lobsters), and support for the Hungarian theatrical producer Eugene Roberts may well have had similar motives. Behind his hard-talking, deal-spinning, public persona, Korda offered a genuinely sympathetic and accommodating response to the plight of the émigré and the exile. As the journalist Paul Marcus recalled in 1953, 'we don't have to tell you how helpful he [Korda] was to everybody who knocked at his door'.[37] Indeed, the sequence in his 1936 film *Things to Come* (based on H. G. Wells's 1933 book *The Shape of Things to Come*) that depicts the fatal plague, 'the wandering sickness' afflicting the post apocalyptic world of the near future, provides a sensitive and highly prophetic vision of the plight of the millions of European refugees who would cross Europe in the next decade.

FOUR
Korda and the Politics
of Representation

Contemporary film criticism identifies the creation of a coherent, on-screen universe, sealed off from the world of the viewers in the stalls, as a central feature of 'classic' western narrative film-making. In this 'fourth-wall cinema', the spectators are invited into the fictional environment of the film, like the child in the sweet shop, on a 'you can look but cannot touch' basis. They are encouraged to see that world as satisfyingly self-sufficient, with the corollary that their own role as part of a collective social organisation, an audience, engaged in a collaborative experience of viewing, is minimised.[1] *Henry VIII*, on the other hand, does not insist (or at least not consistently) on the hermetic integrity of its onscreen world, despite the care with which its Tudor *mise-en-scène* is established. It allows for moments of direct address to the camera, and so for tacit acknowledgement of the role of the spectator 'out there', beyond the screen. It also produces moments of overt, self-referential theatricality – most notably in Laughton's highly knowing, declamatory performance as the King, but also in Elsa Lanchester's ambivalent relationship with the camera – in which, even when it is not spoken to directly, its presence is indirectly acknowledged in implied nods and winks, textual ironies that fly over the heads of the onscreen courtiers to the more 'knowing' spectators beyond. Such features beckon the spectator into collaborative involvement in the idea of the film as a performance, a show put on for their entertainment, rather than a realistic, documentary-style exploration of the private life of a real historical figure.

Critics have tended to read Korda's films as consciously ahistorical, sacrificing serious engagement with political issues in favour of a romanticisation of the past supposedly favoured by the predominantly female audiences attracted to the costume film genre. Korda himself claimed to be aiming for the sort of romanticised historicity evident in the plays of Shakespeare or high opera rather than the 'dry' academicism of the history books. As he was to say of his 1934 feature, *Catherine the Great*: 'One did not want perfect historical detail in films ... film producers had to falsify history as Shakespeare did.'[2] To this end Korda's films, as we shall see, elided the strangeness of the past in favour of recognisable contemporary stereotypes and situations, but this overt use of modern frames of reference did not wholly depoliticise the material. There are momentary allusions in *Henry VIII* to the different perspectives on events available to individuals in the sixteenth century, but they are limited to knowing asides, sufficiently broad to appeal to the superior knowledge of anyone with more than a passing acquaintance with the history of the period. Thus there is a moment of historical irony (and simultaneously a gibe at contemporary American culture) when Paston tries to dissuade Culpeper from fleeing to the New World with the warning, 'North America? ... It's impossible – nothing but a howling wilderness full of howling savages.' And in a similarly ironic vein Henry sums up the likely prospects of his progeny: 'I grant you the daughters show little promise. Mary may grow to wisdom, but Elizabeth will never learn to rule so much as a kitchen.'[3] Such moments produce a veneer of historical authenticity which flatters the audience who can congratulate themselves that they 'know better', but they do little to 'educate' viewers into the nature or preoccupations of Tudor society in the way that Philip Lindsay or the Historical Association hoped. There are also attempts to suggest something of the ritual of the Tudor court. When, for example, the royal bedchamber is prepared for use, swords are thrust under the four-poster, warming-pans are inserted between the sheets, and a good deal of rose-water is cast in all directions. What is created, however, is not a sense of the archaeological reproduction of a lost culture, but merely the addition of a hint of the exotic to an otherwise recognisable and mundane occasion. The phenomenon is at its most awkward in the curious prelude to the council scene in which Henry is told about Catherine Howard's adultery. When the King enters what seems a very small room, all those councillors who are sitting at the table stand up, and all those standing crowded in behind them kneel down. When Henry sits, those who are now standing sit, while those who are kneeling stand up again; the result suggests not dignified Tudor protocol but an attempt at a Mexican wave in a phone box.

Rather than explore the past with any rigour, what the film does is engage with a number of modern debates about England, its culture and contemporary foreign policy, in ways, some of which at least, Tallents and his allies would have approved of. In particular the film offers a view of Englishness that promotes the approved image of the nation both abroad and to domestic audiences, while also pursuing a distinctly conservative political agenda on a number of key issues.

Sue Harper suggests, perceptively, that *Henry VIII* fosters an 'aristocratic–proletarian alliance', encouraging the audience to identify with the King and share his perspective on events. It does so partly, as Sarah Street has observed, through the inclusion of a host of court servants: the barber, Henry's nurse, and especially the kitchen staff, who all talk about Henry in sympathetic, familiar terms, as if they were his personal friends or neighbours – unlike the ministers and courtiers whose relationship with the King is formal, self-interested and dominated by the demands of domestic and international politics.[4] But there is a more general principle at work, too, rooted in the way in which the film seeks to co-opt the audience itself and the processes of cinema-going into its representational strategies.

A number of critics have noted the cultural significance of the roughly simultaneous development, at the turn of the twentieth century, of the picture palace and the department store, two institutions designed to produce and celebrate the display of material commodities on a grand scale. Each, as Jane M. Gaines has put it, offers 'spectacles of plenty'.[5] Just as the new stores brought together the produce of a rapidly globalising economy for the delectation of the affluent middle classes, and offered the prospect of a new, more luxurious lifestyle even to those who could afford only to look at the goods on display, so, it is argued, the cinemas put those affluent lifestyles (drawn from across America as well as from closer to home) on the screen in every provincial town, offering glamorous potential futures to which the ambitious spectator might aspire. One can detect precisely this principle at work in many of the films of the early 1930s, including a number of Korda's own productions. *Wedding Rehearsal* (LFP, 1933), for example, offers its audiences just the kind of opportunities for identification with and aspiration to the lives of its Mayfair-dwelling subjects that Gaines describes. But *Henry VIII*, like a number of the other costume pictures of the period, presents a rather different take on this dynamic of identification. Ostensibly, rather than evoking direct aspiration by suggesting the potential similarities between the onscreen world and the experiences of the audience, Korda's film offers the spectator a more passive relationship with the material pleasures of the onscreen world. It seeks to evoke a sense of wonder, and vicarious pride at the magnificence of the monarchy, and of English history more generally, presenting a series of spectacles to be delighted in and consumed in its executions, weddings, rituals and banquets. The viewer is treated to a sumptuous display of food, lavishly prepared, as the 'pigs, chickens, geese, [and] sheep' brought into the royal kitchens are turned into dishes for the King's table, 'cooked, trimmed, and ready to be consumed'.[6] This is not a lifestyle that the audience could ever hope to share, nor a world that they could ever inhabit, except as distant spectators (as we shall see, a great deal of effort is expended to provide onscreen analogues to the cinema audience in this respect, embedding the latter in the role of witnesses to its narrative and effects). But, crucially, Henry's is presented as a lifestyle that they would not *wish* to share, as, for all its sumptuous material surfaces, so different to modern bourgeois experience, it is in all other respects merely a more burdensome version of their own lives. Henry may be a king, but he is still 'only' a henpecked husband, a man, like the dwellers in the mock-Tudor houses that sprang up in the English suburbs during the 1930s, with a job to do, overburdened with responsibilities and unable to control his own destiny.

The film consequently fluctuates in its opening sequence between a depiction of monarchy as 'special' and one of royalty as 'just like you and me', opting ultimately, after much of the titillation that is central to its appeal as 'behind closed doors' cinema, to stress the latter view.[7] The idea implicit in the film's title that it will provide access to a 'private' world, hitherto denied to public gaze by the passing of time and the dictates of social privilege, is evoked in the opening shots. After two captions wittily summarising the historical context of the first two royal marriages, and setting the tone for the film's take on marital matters,[8] the metaphor of historical knowledge mediated through the written word – the preserve of scholars and the schoolroom – is replaced by the enticing prospect of ostensibly unmediated access to 'history' itself. The screen fades up to a long-shot of Hampton Court Palace, framed through a gateway, which dissolves into a closer shot of the Clock Tower Gate. This image of penetration into the intimate spaces of the palace is taken to its logical extreme in the next shot, showing the innermost sanctum of royal privacy, Henry's bedchamber, and the sovereign's bedhead itself. The voyeuristic thrill that this opening scene is intended to impart is experienced vicariously through the group of giggling ladies-in-waiting who crowd in through the bedchamber door for their own first sight of Henry's nocturnal habitat. The screenplay is unequivocal about the intensity and nature of the pleasure that this visit provides them.

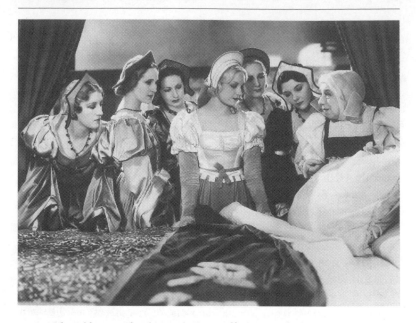

7. *The Old Nurse (Lady Tree) shows off the royal bed.*

The young ladies approach the bed, the Old Nurse leading them. It is a very exciting adventure for the young ladies …

1ST LADY: So that's the King's bed.

NURSE: Yes … (*Slips her hand down the bed.*) And he has not long left it – feel!

1ST LADY: I wonder what he looks like – in bed.

2ND LADY (*a rival beauty*): *You'll* never know![9]

Having pandered to the viewers' voyeuristic tendencies and craving for the exotic in these opening moments, the film ultimately opts for a far more comforting view of royalty, and of the past in general; that it was no different in its emotional essentials to contemporary experience. The trials and tribulations of the King, and the situations through which his life plays out, prove to be remarkably similar to those of the working-class and bourgeois spectators of the 1930s who made up the vast bulk of *Henry VIII*'s audience.[10]

The audience is carefully oriented in this world that is both temporally remote yet comfortably familiar through the treatment of the potentially unsettling scene of Anne Boleyn's execution. Rather than offer an historically 'accurate' representation of what would have been a carefully regulated and socially exclusive event on Tower Green, attended by a select group drawn from the governing classes, the scene is presented as a public spectacle, drawing explicit comparisons with the audience's own experience as cinema-goers.[11] The disturbing strangeness of the event is diminished through a variety of carefully prepared shots and the explicit recasting of Queen Anne as a matinée heroine and the spectators (through whose eyes we view the event) as an audience in search of a good 'weepy' ('HUSBAND: Well, I must admit, she died like a Queen. / WIFE: Yes, and that frock, wasn't it too divine?'; an exchange not in the printed screenplay).

The raised scaffold is carefully framed in the opening shot, taken through an archway that provides a perfect proscenium for the scene to follow. In front of the arch the working-class spectators sit or mill about, beyond it, nearer to the block, are a better class of audience, and the ranks of the guards and musicians. The view is clearly that from the rear stalls. Then, as with the carefully staged penetration of Hampton Court in the opening sequence, we move through a series of shots of the audience, to a more privileged viewpoint from the base of the scaffold. It is from this angle that we will later view Anne herself, self-referentially shot in the manner of a screen heroine (the role was successfully designed to launch the career of Merle Oberon) in head and shoulders shot against a clear sky.

Meanwhile the spectators are shown finding their places and preparing themselves for the event in ways which make the evocation of cinematic metaphors explicit. Indeed, the modern resonances are heightened by the removal from the scene of those remaining distancing elements of Tudor protocol that had been written into the original screenplay. The opening direction for the crowd scenes in the screenplay reads: 'Tower Green with the scaffold and the block. Guests begin to arrive. Officers of the Tower place them according to their ranks.' The scene in the screened version, however, dispenses with such formality and concern for social hierarchy in favour of a more spontaneous, ostensibly democratic situation. The incoming spectators mill about, finding their own way to spare seats, gossiping among themselves, and calling out to their friends ('Here I am, darling!'). Instead of being directed by 'the Officers of the Tower', individuals negotiate their own rules of etiquette and precedence, again explicitly in the cinematic idioms of 1930s England ('Would you mind taking off your hat, madam – we can't see the block.').[12] This conscious exploitation of stereotypical situations, modes and figures lies at the heart of Korda's approach to historical film-making,

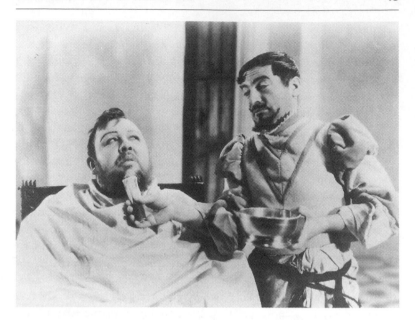

8. 'Something for the weekend?': Henry and the royal barber
exchange pleasantries.

as we have seen. Here indeed was the 'international film', rooted firmly
in the everyday experience of its audiences, wherever they might be.

Elsewhere, Henry's particular experiences, and particularly his experiences of women and marriage, are constantly read against supposedly
'universal' models – in reality the stereotypical positions of English
bourgeois comedy. Notable in this respect is the portrayal of Jane
Seymour (Wendy Barrie) as the kind of dizzy housewife who would
have a long life in situation comedy in both Britain and America. Her
intrusion into the council chamber to ask Henry's advice on the 'really
important' question of which headdress she should wear for her wedding, is played as merely the stereotypical misplaced female interruption
of 'men's talk' in the parlour writ large.

The King's behaviour is interpreted in the light of this wealth of
'common experience' and vice-versa.

CATHERINE [HOWARD]: Do you think he will marry again?
CULPEPER: Who?
CATHERINE: The King.
CULPEPER: Let us hope not! Three failures should convince him that
   he has no gift for the business.

CATHERINE: No, it was the wives who were lacking. The *right* woman could (still) make him happy.

CULPEPER (*laughing*): Every woman thinks herself the right wife for every other woman's husband.[13]

All the characters have their own take on marriage based upon their own experience, and generally expressed in metaphors from their own trades. So, for the barber, 'having a family's like having a shave – once you've started there's no leaving off in the middle'. For the cooks the recipe is somewhat different.

PASTRY COOK: … marriage is like pastry, one must be born to it!

2ND COOK: More like one of these French stews, you never know what you're getting until it's too late!

Henry's limited success in producing a male heir is discussed in the royal kitchens in exclusively culinary terms:

[COOK'S] WIFE: Tried too often, if you ask me; to say nothing of the side dishes – a little bit of this and a little bit of that! What a man wants is regular meals.

COOK: Yes, but not the same joint every night.

WIFE: Oh!

COOK: A man loses his appetite after four courses.

Beneath the surface comedy of these homespun reactions to the royal condition is a more substantial political agenda. The King is presented as a man like any other, subject to the same pressures and urges as his subjects. Shorn in this way of the unique powers that are the prerogative of kingship (and so of political responsibility for the events that befall him), he is presented as a wholly more sympathetic figure. The corollary is, of course, that, since he has to carry the political burdens of the entire nation as well as the personal burdens that all men are heir to, he deserves even greater sympathy rather than envy or resentment from those who serve him. The point is made on a number of occasions, initially in comic mode during the kitchen scene, as the experience of Henry's first four wives is transmuted (through a somewhat laboured extended metaphor) into a martyrdom for Henry himself.

COOK: He got into the soup with Catherine of Aragon, cried stinking fish with Anne Boleyn, cooked Jane Seymour's goose, and gave Anne of Cleves the cold shoulder.

WIFE: God save him! It's no wonder he suffers in the legs.[14]

That kingship is a trial rather than a privilege is emphasised more obviously in the line, delivered with marvellous languor by Laughton as he enters Anne of Cleves's chamber on their wedding night: 'The things I've done for England!' Finally, it is revisited with faux-Shakespearean grandeur, in his lament to Wriothesley: 'Greatness! I would exchange it all to be my lowest groom who sleeps above the stable with a wife who loves him.'[15] Here the kind of socially cohesive ideology underpinning Tallents's agenda for 'the projection of England' (and what Street has identified as Korda's distinctive sense of the bonds between monarchy and the working class) is made explicit.[16]

By universalising the experience of his characters, Korda avoids the close analysis of the specifics of each historical situation ('the deep roots' in his terms) that would expose the real differences between past and present, rich and poor, English and émigré. The 'international film' does indeed appear to present the historical heritage of Englishness, but only by offering the audience a flattering mirror of themselves. The impression that we have gained access to another, otherwise hidden world, and learned something significant about the past is thus entirely illusory. As we shall see, the diplomatic situation in the 1530s is depicted by Korda as a reproduction of the contemporary European hostilities of the 1930s, just as the world of the Tudor court is represented as a reflection of the familiar world of contemporary bourgeois marital humour, in which the exclusively male preserve of the Henrician Privy Chamber with its complex protocols of access and ritual is transformed into the fictionalised suburban bedrooms of contemporary comedy.

ENGLISHNESS, HENRY VIII AND NATIONAL DEFENCE: PAST AND FUTURE POLITICS

Henry VIII promotes a very definite model of Englishness in the officially approved mode of 'plain John Bull' that unites both king and subject. At the bottom of the social scale this English stereotype is represented by the plain-speaking, good-humoured cooks and skivvies in the kitchen scenes, and, more overtly, by the English executioner whose character displays an additional bluntness and belligerence set off perfectly in his disputes with his French superior. As the screenplay makes plain, the two figures are designed to appeal to recognisable national stereotypes: 'They should be contrasting types – the Frenchman

9. *The French and English executioners (Gibb McLaughlin and Sam Livesey).*

very supple and willowy, the Englishman very square and powerful.'[17] The latter, reduced to turning the massive grindstone while the former sharpens his blade, should, according to the script, regard his French counterpart 'with resentment and contempt' when he boasts of his skills, and is as scathing in his dismissal of French qualities as he is proud of those of his own countrymen.

> ASSISTANT: She's an English Queen, isn't she? Well, what's wrong with English steel? And, come to that, what's wrong with an English headsman?
>
> EXECUTIONER: (Ah,) Meaning yourself?
>
> ASSISTANT: Why not? I was good enough to knock off the Queen's five lovers, wasn't I? Then why do they want you over – a Frenchman from Calais? *He spits on the grindstone with savage contempt.*

In this one exchange the film manages to allude simultaneously to the politics of ethnic and national difference, to current international tensions, domestic class conflict and the consequences of industrial depression.

ASSISTANT: ... it's a damned shame, with half the English executioners out of work as it is!

EXECUTIONER (*very angrily*): And *why* are they out of work? Because they are only fit to sever the bull-necks of their countrymen with a butcher's cleaver! But a woman's neck, a Queen's neck – that calls for *finesse*, for delicacy, for *chivalry* (*he kisses his fingertips*) – in one word – a Frenchman!

ASSISTANT: I can think of *another* word!

That the surly English assistant is given the final word, leaving the Frenchman indignant and confounded, suggests where the sympathies of this particular 'international' film surely lie. At a time when the number of unemployed people in Britain had reached 2.75 million, and when civic agitation of the kind that produced the National Hunger March of autumn 1932 was a cause of grave concern to the government, such references were hardly uncontentious.[18] The film seems overtly to be speaking up for the English working man fighting for the right to work, and appears to endorse a patriotic position on protection for British industries. There is, however, an irony adding to both the richness of the comedy and the sharpness of the political edge to this scene. As one significant aspect of industrial unrest in this period was, as we have seen, centred on the film industry itself, and expressed in precisely the kind of anti-alien sentiments voiced by the English executioner, Korda's treatment of the scene is likely to have been at best equivocal. If on one level Korda the populist, anxious to court a patriotic audience and to please the conservative circles in which he wished to move, clearly speaks through the disgruntled English headsman, so also Korda the émigré craftsman and still more, perhaps, Biró the émigré artist and scriptwriter, proud of their superior technical skills and aesthetic principles, speak through the French master with his regard for *finesse* and contempt for the journeyman abilities of the English.

The same qualities of plain-speaking and pragmatic patriotism that characterise the English executioner underlie the representation of King Henry, who is shown rejecting the attractions of similar qualities of *finesse* and delicacy – albeit in a higher register – in the first of the film's council scenes. The King's affinity with artisanal attitudes is signalled here, not only by the sentiments he expresses, but also by the striking pose in which he delivers them, legs apart in the Holbein manner, and with one thumb thrust out at arm's length before him, like a draughtsman thoughtfully sizing up his masterpiece. Craftsman-King and craftsman-

10. *Henry at table: the draughtsman's thumb again.*

executioner are shown to be united in their instinctively blunt response to the problems of international relations. The scene begins with the argument in full-flow:

HENRY: No, Cromwell, if England were as rich as Portugal or as big as Spain you might be right, but this little island of three million souls is no match for all Europe. If these French and Germans stop cutting each other's throats, what's to stop 'em cutting ours?

CROMWELL: Wise diplomacy, Sire.

HENRY: Diplomacy? Diplomacy me foot! [*He stamps to emphasise the point*]. I'm an Englishman; I can't say one thing and mean another [*Extends the thumb, thoughtfully*]. But what I can do is to build ships, ships, and more ships.

CROMWELL: You mean double the fleet?

HENRY: Treble it! Fortify Dover. Rule the Sea!

CROMWELL: To do this will cost us money, Sire.

HENRY: To leave it undone will cost us England. [*He raises the thumb again. Cut to councillors nodding sagely in agreement.*][19]

This much-rewritten scene is fashioned in order not only to reflect Henry VIII's historical role in laying the foundations of the English navy, but also to intervene directly (or as directly as the censors, notoriously sensitive to expressions potentially upsetting to foreign governments, would allow) in contemporary debates about foreign policy.

Underpinning the scene, and the film in general, is a sense of a diplomatic situation in which Europe is locked in a belligerent stand-off between France and Germany (the Habsburg Empire, ruled from Spain, and encompassing the Netherlands and the Holy Roman Empire, is referred to as 'German' throughout), with England somewhat uneasily poised between them, its agenda dictated by the machinations of the continental neighbours. England is portrayed as the peacemaker, and the film repeatedly asserts the need to avoid war through a policy of armed neutrality. The most notable endorsement of this position is offered by the 'mature' Henry towards the end of the film, as he refuses to join either continental power in a war against the other.

> In my youth, in Wolsey's time, I would have accepted one offer or the other. But what's the use of new territories and wars, wars, wars (again)? If those French and Germans don't stop killing (each other), the whole of Europe will be in ruins. I want to compel them to keep peace, peace, peace – and there's nobody in Europe to help me.[20]

The plea for peace and the particular spin put upon it by the earlier demand for 'ships, ships, and more ships' places the film squarely in the middle of the most contentious question of national and international politics in the early 1930s: to disarm or not to disarm in the interests of national security?

In retrospect the whole question of international arms agreements and disarmament has been tarred with the brush of 'appeasement' and seen as short-sighted weakness in the face of Nazi aggression. But in the early 1930s, while no one was sure of the extent of German ambitions (not least the Germans themselves), and with memories of the carnage of the First World War still fresh, the search for a peaceful resolution of international tensions was a project with broad support from most sectors of the political nation. The prospect that another major war would, owing to the technological advances of the previous decade, be still more destructive than the last, was a further spur to the peacemakers' endeavours, and dominated most domestic thinking on the issue at the time.

The apocalyptic scenarios prompted by contemplation of another war centred on the newly enhanced destructive potential of air-power, and particularly on the prospect of a devastating 'knock-out blow' from the air, aimed at civilian populations and involving bombs containing poison gas and other weapons of mass destruction. Such an attack, once launched, would, it was felt, be unstoppable. As Stanley Baldwin told the House of Commons in the course of a speech vividly evoking the horrors of an air war, 'the bomber will always get through'. Any future conflict would thus be even more devastating than the last, as the 'war zone' would extend over a far wider geographical region. Civilisation itself, it was argued, might well not survive. This was the burden of a number of Baldwin's speeches in the period, most notably to the Conservative Party conference of 1933. The nature of modern warfare, he was to reassert in 1936, was such that 'if that fire is ever lighted again on the Continent, no man can tell where the heather will stop burning'.[21] It was a theme to which Korda would allude repeatedly and with increasing directness in his films of the 1930s, most powerfully, perhaps, in *Things to Come* (LFP, 1935), in the sequence in which Everytown is devastated by aerial attack, but also in the Armada film, *Fire Over England* (LFP, 1937, directed by William K. Howard, and produced by Erich Pommer), which, like *Henry VIII*, used admiration for the Tudor navy as a coded call for rearmament. Most obviously, the theme was returned to in the overtly propagandistic *The Lion Has Wings* (LFP, 1939, directed by Michael Powell, Brian Desmond Hurst and Adrian Brunel), which reused footage of Flora Robson as Elizabeth I from the earlier film. Here and elsewhere, the message was the same: the only way to deter such an attack was to prepare adequate defences against it.

During the early 1930s, however, this message was not one that the nation was willing to heed. The consensus among right and left was in favour of collective security and disarmament. Agreements such as the Locarno Treaty of 1925 seemed to confirm the wisdom of such thinking. Only after the unilateral German withdrawal from the Geneva disarmament talks and the League of Nations in October 1933 were Baldwin and his Cabinet colleagues convinced of the need to rearm, and only in November 1933 did they establish a Defence Requirements Committee to consider a detailed programme of military spending. Even then it was widely felt in government circles that public opinion was broadly against rearmament (on the grounds that any military expansion would prompt an arms race and thus make war more rather than less likely) and would need substantial 're-educating' if it was to support significantly increased spending on defence. An indication of the weight of public opinion on the point can, indeed, be gained from the result of the by-election in East Fulham, held on 25 October, two days after *Henry VIII*'s gala launch at the Leicester Square Theatre. The National Government candidate was defeated by an Independent Socialist, John Wilmot, whose manifesto included a call for further and faster disarmament, and who used his victory speech to express the hope that 'the British Government shall give a lead to the whole world by initiating immediately a policy of general disarmament'.[22]

Only a small number of the die-hard Tories (those who were not lionising Hitler as a valuable ally against Soviet communism), those government ministers with direct responsibility for military or naval affairs, and elements of the right-wing press (chiefly Lord Rothermere's *Daily Mail* and Lord Beaverbrook's *Daily Express*) were arguing prior to November 1933 for serious rearmament. These anti-German die-hards were deeply sceptical of Baldwin, their party leader's line, and of the willingness of France and Germany to disarm. Cuthbert Headlam, the Conservative MP for Barnard Castle, recorded in his diary on 14 October 1932 that 'the faddists and clever people' were urging the government 'to make the French to lie down with the Germans', but, he asked, 'do they really think that anything we can say can carry any weight when we have no kind of military, air, or naval power behind us?' On 11 May 1933, Lord Hailsham told the House of Lords that British disarmament was an act of 'courage almost amounting to fool-hardiness'. Fifteen days later Headlam was confiding to his diary that the disarmament negotiations were simply 'mark[ing] time until the time arrives when Germany feels strong enough to go to war again ... but war there will be as certain as eggs are eggs'. Both the *Daily Mail* and the *Daily Express* argued for significant increases in the British bomber fleet to act as a deterrent against German airborne aggression. The call voiced by Laughton's Henry for 'ships, ships, and more ships', was to find an echo in the *Mail*'s headline of November 1933, 'We Need 5,000 War Planes'.[23]

Once freed of his responsibilities as Chancellor of the Exchequer, Winston Churchill began to take a similar line, arguing that the only way to avoid a war was to have a navy and air force sufficiently strong to deter aggression. On 26 May 1932 he published an impassioned article in the *Daily Mail* warning against precipitous disarmament and favouring what he saw as the safer route of allowing the crippling cost of high military expenditure to bring about reductions among the potential combatants, 'naturally'. 'The cause of disarmament', he wrote,

will not be attained by mush, slush, and gush, it will be advanced steadily by the harassing expense of fleets and armies, and by the growth of confidence in a long peace. It will be achieved only when in a favourable atmosphere half a dozen great men, with as many first class powers at their back, are able to lift world affairs out of their present increasing difficulties.[24]

On 17 November 1932 Churchill had written in the *Mail*: 'If Geneva fails, let the National Government propose to Parliament measures necessary to place our Air Force in such a condition of power and efficiency that it will not be worth anyone's while to come here and kill our women and children in the hope that they may blackmail us into surrender.'[25]

Within the Cabinet the debates rumbled on. On 14 March the Under-Secretary for Air, Sir Philip Sassoon, was reiterating 'the need for economy' during the Commons debate on the air estimates, offering a reduction of £340,000 in spending on the air force in addition to the £700,000 reduction announced in the previous year. 'No new units have been formed either at home or abroad during the last year,' he assured his colleagues, 'and no provision is made for new units in the present estimates.' Against this Churchill argued 'not to have an adequate air force in the present state of the world is to compromise the foundations of national freedom and independence ... we should be well advised to concentrate upon our air defences with great vigour'.[26]

Korda's decision to have Laughton's Henry VIII call for the fortification of Dover and 'ships, ships, and more ships' to allow him to 'compel' the French and Germans to 'peace, peace, peace' was then not merely a passive reflection of contemporary events – a transcription of the diplomatic situation of the early 1930s on to the history of the 1530s. It was an active intervention in the debates conducted in Parliament and Cabinet, and in the wider forum of the popular press, in favour of the line argued by Churchill and the anti-German die-hards. It is tempting to see the influence of Korda's fellow London Films director Captain A. C. N. Dixey in all this. Dixey was a long-time opponent of Stanley Baldwin and the mainstream Tory leadership, and was so extreme an advocate of the die-hard position that even Churchill was later to describe him as a 'crack pot'.[27] But to see Korda as simply the cat's paw of his Tory colleague is to belittle his own appreciation of and contribution to contemporary political debates, a contribution based upon his experiences over the previous fifteen years.

Korda's motives in promoting a Churchillian line on rearmament

plausibly involved a mixture of idealism and shrewd commercial calculation. His attempts to court, and subsequently to ally himself with,
Churchill combined two of the director's major preoccupations: his desire
to win the approval of the political and cultural elite in Britain (and
thereby establish London Film Productions as an 'international' concern
firmly embedded in the loam of British middle-brow culture), and his
own opposition to Nazism. As a refugee from right-wing persecution
himself, and someone in regular touch with the many fugitives from
Germany who sought employment in the British film industry between
1930 and 1933, he was, of course, well placed to appreciate the dangers
posed by the new Nazi regime in Berlin. His opposition to Nazism and
political dictatorship generally was, in fact, a consistent theme in many
of his films of the 1930s, and was certainly sincerely held. (It was Korda,
for example, who first suggested to Charlie Chaplin that he exploit the
physical similarities between his Tramp persona and Hitler in a satirical
film, a suggestion that was to lead to one of the most effective cinematic
attacks on Nazism, *The Great Dictator* [United Artists, 1940].)[28] Churchill
therefore represented a kindred spirit as well as someone who might
bring further glamour to London Films' operations and provide an
avenue into the cultural establishment. The latter were not, however,
inconsiderable factors in the equation. While Churchill was a relatively
marginal figure, politically speaking, during his 'wilderness years' in the
early 1930s, estranged from both the leadership of his own party and the
National Government by his views on India and rearmament, he was
none the less an important member of the British cultural elite. He was
a flamboyant yet quintessentially English figure, whose star remained
very much in the ascendant overseas, especially in the all-important
American market, as his tours of the States in 1929 and 1931–32 effectively demonstrated. In mobilising London Films to the Churchillian
cause over rearmament, then, Korda was pursuing a potential ally with
much to offer him in both cultural and commercial terms.[29]

Interestingly, the subtle, coded support offered by Henry's comments
on the need for a strong navy (they had to be subtly coded to avoid the
blue pencil of censors acutely anxious to avoid offending the German
government) does not seem to have attracted Churchill's attention. He
may well not even have seen the film on its first release. Certainly on the
one occasion when he definitely did view it, at a private showing at
Chartwell in 1935, he made no mention of having seen it before. Indeed,
he did not seem to think much of it at all, finding Korda's later costume
picture, *The Rise of Catherine the Great*, much more interesting. 'We had

a demonstration last Sunday of the photophone down here,' he wrote
to his wife Clementine on 18 January.

> All the servants and some of the neighbours attended. We had three
> films, including *Henry VIII* and *Catherine the Great*. It was marvellous.
> I did not mind *Henry VIII*, and I thought *Catherine* really superb. I have
> since read a book about her, and, although they have taken liberties with
> the history, the film in the main is true. I think it is a very fine show.[30]

By 1934, however, Korda had followed up the implied overture represented by *Henry VIII* with a more practical commercial approach. When,
precisely, Korda first met Churchill is not clear from their surviving
papers. The reminiscences of others variously suggest an initial meeting
'in a pub near Isleworth Studios' in 1934, or at John Loder's brother-in-
law's house.[31] Kulik suggests that it was through the offices of Churchill's
factotum Brendan Bracken that Korda first met Robert Vansittart, Winston Churchill and other Conservative Party members in the early 1930s,
and places the first meeting with Churchill (arranged by the latter's son,
Randolph, who was already working in the publicity department of
London Films) in the Isleworth pub in September 1934. But Korda's
links with the Tories, and with the anti-German die-hards in particular,
clearly pre-date this meeting by a considerable margin, as we have seen.
He knew both William Brownlow (the future Lord Lurgan) and Captain
Dixey well enough in 1932 to ask them to join the board of directors of
London Films. Indeed, it looks very much as if both men had already
been 'purged' from the board (their usefulness over, once they had
introduced Korda to more influential figures in the party?) by the time
that Churchill was brought on board.[32]

What is clear is that Korda quickly bought up the film rights to
Churchill's biography of Marlborough, and offered him contracts to
write scripts for a film celebrating George V's silver jubilee and the series
of 'shorts' floated in 1934. These films, like so many others projected or
contracted by Korda in these years, were never made, but effectively kept
Churchill associated with London Films, and on the payroll, through the
mid-1930s. After 1934, Churchill was a regular visitor to London Films'
Grosvenor Street offices.[33] And, once established, the alliance between
producer-director and politician was to prove firm, long-lasting, and
mutually advantageous, leading to effective collaboration during the
1939–45 war, and to Korda's knighthood (as the film industry's first
recipient of the honour) in June 1942.[34]

Korda's assistance to Churchill took various forms. As well as offering him a valuable financial lifeline during his wilderness years, the producer was able to give his one-time employee direct practical help once he returned to the centre of government. A number of Korda's films offered coded (and often not-so-coded) support for the Churchillian line on foreign policy. Even before the overtly propagandistic *The Lion Had Wings* (1939) went into production, *The Scarlet Pimpernel* (1934) and *Things to Come* (1935) had both, like *Henry VIII*, contained powerful arguments against appeasing the European dictators, calls for British rearmament, and encouragements for greater American involvement in international efforts to limit German ambitions in Europe. Significantly, these films appeared at a time when the political agenda of the majority of British studios was predominantly Baldwinite, leading to the production of pro-appeasement films such as the trio of George Arliss vehicles made by Gaumont British, *The Iron Duke* (1935, directed by Victor Saville), *East Meets West* and *His Lordship* (both 1936 and directed by Herbert Mason), each of which stressed the need for international reconciliation.[35]

Paula Ringer, the only other writer to date to take Korda seriously as a consistent propagandist in the 1930s, offers an interesting, but I think misleading, reading of the role of *Henry VIII* in Korda's 'propaganda campaign'. Her suggestion, published in a short, stimulating article in *Classic Images* in 1995, that Laughton's Henry is himself an allusion to the evils of dictatorship, rather than a representation of a Churchillian patriotic opposition to 'foreign' tyranny, seems to me a misreading of the final scenes. Rather than asking the viewer to reflect critically upon Henry's violent history, I suspect that the final sequence of the film seeks to evoke genuine sympathy for the ageing monarch, deflecting attention away from his former crimes with its comically-inflected depiction of marital strife (for more on this theme, see the following chapter). But Ringer's general conclusion that Korda spent the 1930s 'struggling against the rising tide of fascism by making strongly pro-democratic films, which, unlike most propaganda, happened to be quite good', seems shrewd.[36]

The first of these 'political' films, *The Scarlet Pimpernel* (LFP, 1934), was ostensibly directed by Harold Young, but was produced by Korda in the typically 'hands on' manner that was to infuriate so many of his directors. It reunited many of the team that made *Henry VIII*, including the writers Biró and Wimperis (augmented by Robert Sherwood and Sam Behrman),[37] and many of the themes of the earlier film are revisited, not least its preoccupation with notions of Englishness and hostility to dictatorship. As Ringer suggests, the film offers a warning of the political consequences when a liberal, democratic elite loses contact with its people. 'We've been too detached from reality all our lives,' observes the Count de Tournay (O. B. Clarence), as he awaits the guillotine with his fellow aristocrats. 'That's what caused the Revolution. If we'd only had eyes to see our own follies, we shouldn't be here now, waiting to be shaved by the "national razor".' The revolutionary state that has swept away de Tournay and his kind is presented as a regime of 'damnable, useless cruelty', a system built upon repression and terror. As Robespierre (Ernest Milton) tells Chauvelin (Raymond Massey at his gaunt, reptilian, best): 'Our generals in the field know that to lose the battle means the guillotine.' For Robespierre's France, of course, read Hitler's Germany, an analogy drawn so closely that one half expects Chauvelin's soldiers to goosestep. As the newspaper read by the Prince of Wales (played by a young-looking Nigel Bruce, warming up for his role as Dr Watson to Basil Rathbone's Sherlock Holmes with an engaging display of bumbling amiability) declares, Robespierre is 'the self-styled Dictator of France', responsible for crimes that, although largely left unstated, reflect the oppressive policies of the early Nazi years, and effectively foreshadow the greater horrors to come. As Bruce's Prince warns Lady Blakeney, 'if a country goes mad, it has the right to commit *every* horror within its own walls'.[38]

Central to the depiction of revolutionary oppression in *The Scarlet Pimpernel* is the public execution, an event which, as in *Henry VIII*, dominates the early sequences of the film. Again, as in the earlier picture, the depiction of the audience at these grotesque events is carefully handled, both to suggest a political point and to involve the cinema audience vicariously in the event (although there are none of the devices that humanise Henry and seek to distract attention from his political crimes in the later film). The row of women who sit knitting as the guillotine goes to work have many of the same functions as the crowds milling into the seats on Tower Green at Anne Boleyn's execution, albeit with darker overtones. They are both a symbol of a society gone mad, and a mirror of our own culpability as spectators. As the blade falls, they briefly look up from their needles to witness the blow, let out a brief cheer, and then resume their labours, laughing. Behind the comedy of their synchronised responses lies a serious interest in the capacity of a people to countenance the brutality of a repressive regime, to connive in its operation, and even to see it as a source of entertainment. These women, like the symbolic married couple who go to see Queen Anne beheaded, suggest the ease with which individuals can be converted into a paying public, eager to witness and enjoy political murder. So easily, these sequences suggest, is tyranny naturalised. And, if the audiences of the 1930s were in any doubt that the same could be said of their own culture, the films draw, as we have seen, an overt parallel between the onscreen and cinema audiences through their behaviour, and their inane 'modern' responses to the event ('Poor Anne Boleyn … she died like a Queen./Yes, and that frock, wasn't it too divine?'). What had initially been a comforting reassurance about the familiarity of the past becomes, by the end of the scene, a troubling reminder of the dangers of political acquiescence.

Opposing this vision of a repressive revolutionary regime and its quiescent subjects is set Sir Percy Blakeney (Leslie Howard)'s personal heroism, and the notion of modest patriotic Englishness for which he stands. Against the dictatorship and cult of personality of Robespierre is set the collaborative enterprise of the Pimpernel's network of agents which smuggles aristocrats to the Channel ports: a well organised team of men sharing in the risks and the responsibility for their own good works (when one of his lieutenants affirms to him the importance of 'your work', Blakeney gently corrects him, 'our work'). Yet each remains, characteristically, modestly anonymous, like his leader, the definitive self-effacing Englishman who adopts the persona of an effete non-combatant rather than enjoy the public adoration that his heroism inspires. 'Look, Marguerite, England!' is the film's final line, spoken by Blakeney to his wife as their ship nears Dover. And it is England that is the film's real protagonist, lionised as the land of freedom and moral courage – most obviously in the version of John of Gaunt's 'this other Eden' speech from Shakespeare's *Richard II* quoted by Blakeney to Chauvelin during their final confrontation. This eulogy ends with Leslie Howard's splendidly modulated bathos: ' … this blessed plot, this earth, this realm, this England … Oh, demm me, I forget the rest.'[39] If bathos can ever be heroic, it is surely so here.

Korda's version of Englishness is, however, 'international' enough, detached enough, to allow for the recognition of its own contradictions, and to play one stereotypical model against another. *The Scarlet Pimpernel* is rescued from too great a degree of seriousness by remarks such as that uttered by one of the Prince of Wales's entourage in the opening sequence, as he denounces the latest French atrocity: 'Well, what can you expect of a lot of foreigners with no sporting instincts? Gad, if it wasn't for our fox-hunting and our pheasant-shooting, I daresay we should be cruel too.'

And yet, of course, for all its disavowal of the 'foreign' cult of personality, of dictatorship and all its works, Korda's vision of heroism none the less affirms the need for inspirational leadership, for the kind of 'great men, with first class powers at their back' whom Churchill had argued were the only guarantors of a lasting peace. The Pimpernel's men are a team, but they are held together by his commanding example, and by obedience to him. 'It'll be the first time we ever disobeyed him,' Sir Andrew Ffoulkes (Anthony Bushell) tells Lady Blakeney, when he agrees to take his men back to France to rescue Blakeney from Chauvelin's trap.

There are similar ambivalences in *Things to Come*, the next Korda film to engage overtly with such issues, principally in the sequence involving 'the Chief', the petty, Mussolini-like gangster (played by Ralph Richardson) who rules the devastated Everytown with his ramshackle air force of cannibalised bi-planes and ultimately impotent military posturing. The Chief is an indictment of both the intellectual and political bankruptcy of continental fascism, with its surface allure to communities in search of strong leadership (it is his 'firm action' in shooting a victim of 'the wandering sickness' that wins him the support of the demoralised citizens of Everytown, just as his long, futile war with the Hill People maintains his authority). But again, as with the Pimpernel's benign autocracy, what the film finally offers in place of fascism is only another, more benevolent version of strong leadership. It is 'the Dictatorship of the Air', the international cabal of technocrats based in Basra, that liberates Everytown, through an aerial bombardment with 'the gas of peace' – a 'liberal' variation of the bomber-borne carnage visited on the city at the outbreak of the great war in the film's opening movement. The alternative to dictatorship is not liberal democracy and the spirit of disarmament, but the leadership of a Churchillian man of vision, crucially one whose instincts are for peace rather than war. As Mrs Richardson, Merle Oberon's character in *The Lion Has Wings*, put it, Britain was prepared to fight, if it had to, for 'Truth, Beauty, and Fair Play ... and kindness'. (The film may not have been the Korda–Biró–Wimperis writing team's finest hour, but Graham Greene's caustic verdict that its message 'as a statement of war aims ... leaves the world beyond Roedean still expectant' seems a little harsh.)[40] Again the message seems to be that the virtuous folk need to be as well-armed and resolutely led as the fascists if they are to prevail.

The idea is repeated in the unambiguously anti-Hitler stance of *That Hamilton Woman* (1941), shot in black-and-white in six weeks at the General Service studios in Hollywood. Here again the scenario is one in which England faces a powerful continental oppressor with indomitable resolve ('You cannot make peace with dictators. You have to destroy them. Wipe them out!' declares Lord Nelson [Laurence Olivier] to the Lords of the Admiralty.) Again the answer to dictatorship is the resolution of a Nelson, and it is strong defensive measures, not a collective turn towards disarmament, that will ensure a final peace ('There are always men who, for the sake of their insane ambition want to destroy what other people build, and therefore this tiny little bit [of the globe, i.e. Britain] has to send out its ships again and again to fight those who want to dictate their will to others'). The film's obviously propagandistic agenda was to lead to Korda being summoned before the Senate Foreign Relations Committee, which was investigating covert British attempts to 'incite [America] to war' (a not unreasonable allegation, given such obvious statements of the need for America to abandon isolationism as Sir William Hamilton's claim that 'we fought with no allies, the whole of Europe in deadly fear', or Nelson's declaration to the King of Naples, 'we [England] can't protect all Europe', itself a variant of the sentiments expressed by Laughton's Henry VIII: 'I want to compel them [France and Germany] to keep peace, peace, peace – and there's nobody in Europe to help me'). Ultimately, the Japanese attack upon Pearl Harbor was to spare him the ordeal of an interrogation.[41]

If Korda was happy to make films that furthered British diplomatic efforts, he was also prepared *not* to make those that threatened to hinder them. His decision, taken in the late 1930s, not to pursue plans to make the projected film of the war memoirs of T. E. Lawrence, *Revolt in the Desert*, has been put down to a request from Churchill not to do anything that would unsettle British relations with Turkey while the European situation was so precariously balanced.[42]

More practical still in its contribution to British policy was Korda's role as a 'courier' for Churchill during the war years, and the assistance that his New York office was able to offer to British secret service agents during the 1940s. At the time, the director received considerable criticism for his decision to relocate from Denham to America in 1940, but it is clear in retrospect that rather more was involved than a reluctance to contribute to the home front. In addition to giving him a plausible reason for numerous transatlantic flights, Korda's new base in New York provided a cover and a 'clearing house for information' for members of British Security Coordination (BSC), a covert operation established in 1940 under the leadership of the Canadian businessman William Stephenson and Sir Connop Guthrie (in his peacetime incarnation, an executive of the Prudential Assurance and board member of London Films), dedicated to countering German propaganda activities in the USA and encouraging America to enter the war on the side of the Allies. The precise degree of co-operation between Korda and the secret services has never been clearly established, but it is highly suggestive that, once victory was achieved, not only did Stephenson sell his British film company, Sound City Films, to Korda, but Sir Claud Dansey, the Head of MI6, was to join the board of London Films, and a number of his former officers were to find employment within the organisation. It is perhaps going too far to suggest that Korda went to the USA in 1940 *in order* to further British propaganda efforts there; there were sound commercial and practical reasons for relocating to Hollywood at the time. But, once in America, it is clear that he 'did his bit' – and perhaps a bit more – with the particular resources that he had to hand, enough at least to arouse the hostility of Lord Haw-Haw (the Nazi propagandist was to denounce him, not unflatteringly, perhaps, as 'the Disraeli of British films'). His knighthood, bestowed at a time when he, like many of Hollywood's British 'expatriates', was the recipient of considerable press criticism for deserting the home front, seems to have been a tacit acknowledgement of that fact.[43]

FIVE

Marriage, Sex and Gender: Relationships in *Henry VIII*

WIVES

As I suggested in Chapter 4, there is a clear attempt, during her brief appearances in *Henry VIII*, to 'launch' Merle Oberon as a romantic star. Oberon – who started life in Bombay as Estelle Merle O'Brien Thompson, moved to Europe and became first Queenie Thompson and then Merle O'Brien, before finally (in keeping with her role as the 'exotic' element in the London Films stable) becoming Merle Oberon – enjoys a special relationship with the camera in the film.[1] It lingers over her features and holds her face in view from a number of advantageous angles, both in the scenes in her chamber, and, most effectively, as she demurely mounts the scaffold at her execution (the contrast with the presentation of Henny Porten's Anne in Lubitsch's *Anna Boleyn*, who goes to her death in a plain smock, playing the scene for all its desperate emotional resonances, is striking). Oberon's performance also offers a knowing acknowledgement of her own role as 'a beauty'. She is shown in situations that focus attention upon her face and figure (looking into mirrors, adjusting her hair, commenting upon her own appearance). The observation that she will be known to history as 'Anne *sans tête*', spoken as the camera holds a reverential shot of her face, draws attention to her looks, while the further remark that it is a shame 'to lose a head like this', delivered with a half-smile of regret, might have been intended as a reference to the tragic circumstances of her death, but just as effectively highlights the suggestion that her particular head is so attractive that no one would wish to lose it. Indeed, delivered as she looks thoughtfully into a mirror, the line suggests a degree of self-satisfaction at her own beauty somewhat at odds with the tragic mood of the moment. Likewise, there is a half-smile on her lips as she speaks a variation of the historical Anne Boleyn's observation that the executioner's task will be less painful as 'I have such a little neck, haven't I?' Spoken as the camera holds a view of her head and shoulders, the length of her neck accentuated by her low-cut dress, the addition of the final, ahistorical 'haven't I?' turns the remark from a plea for pathos into a cue for aesthetic appreciation. 'Yes, you have,' the shot invites the viewer to reply.

In its treatment of both Anne Boleyn and Catherine Howard (and their anti-type, the 'ugly' Anne of Cleves, performed – again, self-referentially – against type by Elsa Lanchester), the film offers a textbook exposition of Laura Mulvey's thesis concerning the representation of the male gaze in classic narrative cinema.[2] Masculinity is indeed, as Mulvey argued, associated with active seeing, with the voyeuristic look (and hence with the audience's own perspective), as both Henry and the camera view his prospective brides with an eye to their physical desirability, while the female is displayed as the passive recipient of that gaze, fragmented into an agglomeration of glamorised (or in Lanchester's case, comically unglamorised) body parts: face, neck, hands, torso, all shown in emphatic close-up. But *Henry VIII* also offers an alternative version of this so-called 'scopophilic' effect. While Lanchester's Anne of Cleves is all too aware of the power of the male gaze, and refashions her appearance to deter it, Laughton's Henry is himself the object of predatory, voyeuristic looking, and the subject of visual fragmentation in the course of the film. It is *his* 'private life', after all, that the viewer has been invited to observe, his bedchamber into which we have already transgressively penetrated in the opening sequence. And in a number of subsequent scenes the King, like Oberon's Anne, is presented to the viewer as a spectacle for amusement or delight, shown combing his hair, examining his face in mirrors, and being dressed and undressed, his hands, face and bare feet fetishised by close-ups as tokens of his vulnerable, desiring and desirable body.

As he sits at table, tearing at the chicken, or strips off his jacket to take part in the wrestling (the latter scene was given particular importance by Laughton himself in interviews as one in which the King is portrayed as an impressive physical specimen), Henry is held up as the object of general observation, the subject of admiring, anxious or embarrassed comments from his male courtiers. As he parades through the gardens with his young son in his arms, displaying the fruits of his fertility before his retinue of female admirers, he is the subject of giggling speculation from the younger women, and then of comic deflation as the Nurse (played with admirable feistiness by Lady Tree) rebukes him for bringing the child out in the hot sun. Finally, through the character of Catherine Howard, the audience is invited to see Henry vicariously as the object

11. *'Such a little neck': Anne Boleyn (Merle Oberon).*

of desire – not primarily for his personal qualities, but for the avenue
to wealth and advancement that he would represent for 'the *right* woman'
who knows how to handle him. In this way Laughton's king is thoroughly
feminised in Mulvey's terms, presented as another desirable object in the
camera's promiscuous gaze, the passive subject of another's fantasies
about 'a good marriage'.

The film, while appearing to be very conventional, even primitive, in its sexual politics, is, then, actually more subtle and nuanced than it first appears. A narrative that is, ostensibly, about marital strife, presented from the viewpoint of a much-married and long-suffering male protagonist, actually offers its spectators the opportunity to witness, and explore vicariously, the experiences of a number of different female characters, all of whom have to negotiate, and attempt to survive, marriage to a uniquely 'difficult' husband. A series of case studies of dysfunctional marriages (and, in one case at least, a strategy for escaping it) is presented in the guise of Henry's last five brides. There is the abandoned wife and (probably) innocent victim of male violence (Anne Boleyn); the conventional but out of her depth 'ordinary housewife' determined to treat her elevation to royal status as if it were an entirely mundane bourgeois experience (Jane Seymour); then the two far shrewder, self-contained 'strong women' (Anne of Cleves and Catherine Howard), each in her own way using Henry as a means to another, truly desirable object. Finally, there is Catherine Parr, the fussy, domineering mother figure who reprises the role of the Nurse of the first half of the film, and takes all responsibility for his well-being from her infirm, incapable spouse. In its exploration of this range of female experiences of – and responses to – marriage, the film has as much to say about the trials of being a wife as it does about Henry's legendary 'husbandry'. And what it says is far from encouraging.

Almost all of the sexual relationships 'above stairs' in the courtly world of *Henry VIII* are dysfunctional in one way or another, blighted by the conflicting imperatives of politics or the King's capricious desires. Henry's own grotesquely misjudged marriages are the chief examples of this principle, but the relationships between Catherine Howard and Culpeper, and (even if only temporarily) Anne of Cleves and Peynell are also cases in point. Desire is everywhere misplaced and consequently frustrated. The ladies-in-waiting who crowd into the royal bedchamber in the opening scene in pursuit of a glimpse of Henry's still warm bed, aspire (hopelessly as it turns out) to share that bed with him, whether as his mistress or his queen. Such foolish ambitions seem the best hope of love on offer in a court seemingly populated almost exclusively by hordes of women in their twenties and sage male counsellors close to retirement age. In the only two ostensibly evenly matched pairings, hopes are blighted from the outset. When lovers meet, their sightlines, like their ambitions, rarely, if ever, converge, even when they kiss.

When we first see Culpeper and Catherine together on the riverbank, they are physically close (his head in her lap, and later held close to her chest), but there is no meeting of hearts or minds. She, dreaming of the crown and of being the one woman who 'could (still) make him [Henry] happy', looks upwards and out of shot towards her imagined future, while he stares longingly up at her half-turned face. It is a visual motif that will be repeated in their fraught meeting in the King's chamber later in the film. There she (her eyes darting from her wringing hands to the King's bed and back again) admits to Culpeper that he was right: no amount of wealth or influence can compensate for the absence of love, while he stands, back to camera, staring gloomily into the fireplace. The motif returns again in their final scene together. As Henry plays cards with one of his few male courtiers, Catherine, embroidering a sampler, looks eagerly out of shot towards a group of dancers. Culpeper, standing behind the King, stretches to get a view of her, never taking his eyes from the back of her head, seemingly desperate to catch her eye. Their moments of onscreen intimacy are similarly always snatched in passing, fraught with frustration or the fear of discovery, like the clipped 'I adore you' that Catherine half-whispers as they dance, with Henry looking on, just before the fateful privy council meeting that will reveal their infidelity to the King.

Anne of Cleves and Peynell must also suffer a clandestine love, frustrated by circumstances for as long as the film follows their story. In their case the ending is a happy one, as Anne is able ingeniously to secure both a divorce from the King and a role for Peynell as the steward of her estate. But, crucially, the film never shows them together enjoying that happy future. Peynell does not reappear after Anne's divorce has been agreed, she alone returns briefly in the penultimate scene to advise Henry to marry Catherine Parr. Consequently, the abiding image of the above stairs court is of frustrated sexual relationships, and the only affectionate interactions between men and women are not those between husbands and wives, but between son and surrogate mother (Henry and the Nurse – note, for example, their touching concern for each other in the sequence in Prince Edward's nursery) and brother and surrogate sister (Henry and Anne of Cleves after their divorce).

Below stairs, however, it is a different story. The royal kitchens provide a model of harmonious social and sexual relations on an implausibly large scale. Amid scenes of Rabelaisian culinary activity, designed both to arouse and vicariously to satisfy the appetite (as both Kulik and Harper note, sexual appetite and frustration are, rather predictably, associated with the consumption of food in the film),[3] we are treated to a vision of marital relationships that are harmonious, apparently mutually satisfying and, above all, prodigiously productive. An amazingly high percentage of the kitchen staff seems to consist of married couples, each of which works as a team. The pastry cook and his wife, the carver and his spouse, the fish-cook and his: all, as we have seen, exchange knowing and slightly risqué banter about events above stairs, attesting to their own seemingly highly satisfactory sex-lives ('CARVER: I think a man should try for another son or two – If he is a king, eh, Wife? / HIS WIFE: Yes, my man. [*laughs suggestively*] And even if he is *not* a king!').[4] They offer in their (not entirely convincing) chirpy, working-class accents, the 'natural' model of marital relationships from which the King has evidently strayed, lured away by his own misplaced desires and the dictates of state into ever more unworkable and unsatisfactory couplings, as barren of offspring as they are of love.

SONS AND LOVERS

Given this largely acerbic treatment of Henry's marital history, it is curious that the film has attracted a good deal of comment for its apparently frank treatment of sexual issues. Sue Harper has suggested that, like all of Korda's films of the 1930s, *Henry VIII* 'gave class themes an irresistible resonance by combining them with the celebration of sexual love'. Simon Callow included 'sexual naughtiness' among the characteristically 'Korda elements' that made the film so successful. And both the publicity material and the earliest reviews commented on the film's 'deliciously risqué passages' and 'suggestive comedy', stressing the sexual appetites of its royal protagonist as a major element in its appeal ('History's most amorous ruler! A match for any man ... the master of any woman!' John Gamme's review in *Film Weekly* talked of Laughton 'drawing a full-blooded portrait of the gross, sensual monarch in whom lust and the satisfaction of vanity are the ruling passions'). Even when it was reissued in 1950, the film was advertised in Chicago with the slogan 'Rumours, Scandals, Shame! What a King! What a lover! What a Man!'[5]

The film does indeed affect a knowingness on the subject of sex, evident in the risqué asides that litter the dialogue, as, for example, when the gentlewomen talk their way suggestively down the baby prince's body, noting his resemblance to his royal father, before being interrupted in the interests of propriety by Henry himself before they reach the princely genitals.

3RD LADY: His father's hand too! And his deep chest! And, see, the
same legs. And the same ...

HENRY: Madam! Not before the child![6]

But the implied sophistication is, in its protagonist at least, entirely
superficial. As Kulik notes, there are very clear limits to the kind of
'naughtiness' the film will entertain. Korda's approach was 'coy rather
than subtle or suggestive, and ... relied on the sexual *immaturity* of the
audience'.[7] Korda himself spoke of the characteristic reticence evident
in the English portrayal of sexual matters.

> Your French audience is ready for a great deal more frankness and
> breadth in the statement of a sex situation than the English. But that is
> no reason why British films with sex themes or incidents should not be
> enjoyed in France. If anything in the treatment strikes a Frenchman as
> being prim and proper or discreet to the point of absurdity, by his lights,
> he will still accept it because it is British, if the whole character of the
> film is English.[8]

Kulik is probably closer to the mark in seeing the 'quite naive'
treatment of sexuality in the film as more a product of the director's
habitual strategy than a specific response to English sensibilities.

> Korda had taken a titillating subject, cleaned it up, played it for laughs,
> and made it wholly acceptable to audiences everywhere. The glamour
> and pageantry, the pretty girls, and Laughton's performance merely
> enhanced the subject's more basic appeal to cautious, but inhibited people
> who wanted to see a 'sex romp' where the emphasis was on the 'romp'
> not the 'sex'.[9]

In part the film's coyness was a consequence of the notoriously strict
British censorship laws of the period that prevented any overt treatment
of sexually explicit scenes or dialogue. The rigorous regulation of public
representations of sexuality was to foster that particularly British attitude
towards sex in mainstream comic theatre and cinema remarked upon by
Korda, and which was to find its last, triumphant fling in the *Carry On*
films of the 1960s and early 1970s before the relaxation of this form of
censorship sounded its death-knell in the cinemas in the late '70s.

In the 1930s the cinema was still firmly in the grip of a regulatory
regime administered on behalf of the British Board of Film Censors by
its two chief script censors, Colonel J. C. Hanna and Miss N. Shortt.
These two redoubtable individuals, the former an ex-Royal Artillery

officer in his sixties and the latter the daughter of the Board's president, Edward Shortt, were notoriously idiosyncratic in their judgements. As Jeffrey Richards has shown, as well as habitually rejecting the use of words thought to be offensive, ranging from 'gigolo' or 'nymphomaniac', to such seemingly innocuous terms as 'twerp', 'privy' or 'nuts', the censors were also apt to make less predictable interventions in the dialogue and plotlines of the scenarios put before them. Thus the short comic film *Tell Me if It Hurts* (directed by Richard Massingham, Imperial Sound Studios, 1934) was initially denied a certificate on the grounds that it was 'offensive to the dental profession', while the writers of another light comedy, *To Brighton with a Bird* (later retitled as the notionally less salacious *To Brighton with Gladys* [George King Productions, 1933]) were memorably told that 'the scene of the penguin getting drunk must be carefully handled'.[10]

In such an environment scriptwriters, especially those working on films with marital themes, or 'backstage dramas' such as *Henry VIII* – both of which had been singled out for criticism in recent BBFC annual reports – clearly had to be circumspect.[11] But the impact of censorship is only part of the story. What *Henry VIII* offers is a novel variation on a very familiar view of sexuality, and of male sexuality in particular, part of a tradition that has enjoyed a long ascendancy in British marital comedy in literature and theatre as well as on film. In this form of comedy, male power and sexual desire accommodate themselves (to themselves as much as to anything else) by presenting themselves as impotence or inadequacy, while projecting real anxieties on to peripheral characters and symbolic situations. In the kind of comfortable stereotyping in which this comedy deals, the subject-hero is always immature, awkward, comically embarrassed by the prospect of sex and when in the company of desirable or desiring women, but is always portrayed as essentially honest in his motivations and (almost always) is ultimately successful in his quest for love. Conversely, the rival lovers are always more handsome, mature, worldly-wise and conventionally masculine; but they are also insincere, ultimately unsatisfying to know and finally defeated in their ambitions. It generally turns out that the heroine has really preferred the hero (George Formby over George Clooney) all along, and would have said so much earlier, if only he had been brave enough to ask. Of course, such a world-view can work only if sexuality is kept eternally arrested at the adolescent stage, restricted to suggestion and innuendo, and consummation is deferred until beyond the final credits, the fade-out coming on the first and only chaste clinch the couple enjoys, in order to save the day, the censor's blue pencil and the hero's blushes.[12]

When, as in *Henry VIII*, this comic model is applied to historically and politically sensitive material, the result is not really to 'reveal the pervasive sexual innocence of Henry VIII', but something rather more pernicious.[13] The film's treatment of sexuality is anything but innocent, and its suggestive innuendo works consistently towards a sustained portrayal of the King as a victim rather than the perpetrator of violence and brutality, a man whose natural appetites and sense of political duty combine to lead him into a string of increasingly unfortunate encounters with clever women who outwit and humiliate him. (The process is essentially the same as that effected in the music-hall song 'I'm 'Enery the Eighth, I am', in which the much-married King is comically metamorphosed into merely the latest 'victim' of the predatory, if bizarrely selective, serial-wife: 'the widder next door'.)[14] London Films' pressbook for *Henry VIII*, while presenting the King's murderous instincts admiringly in the tones of grotesque comedy ('Every woman got it in the neck, eventually'; 'When he got tired of a wife, he just knocked her block off'), none the less strove to present the King as ultimately the victim, rather than the instigator of his own marital history ('Respectable Catherine, Ambitious Anne, Youthful Jane, Wily Anne, Coquettish Catherine, Shrewish Katheryne: Poor Henry!'). While he may have done monstrous things, the press releases suggest, he was in reality no different from any other poor, henpecked spouse ('The King is shown as a man with human, lovable qualities, and with as many domestic difficulties as any husband who married six times').[15]

The two wives who do not readily fit the model of the 'difficult' wife are, as Karol Kulik has noted, dismissed to the margins of the story, Catherine of Aragon being reduced to a comic aside in the opening caption (' ... she was a respectable woman. So Henry divorced her') and Jane Seymour, restricted to a brief appearance as a 'stupid' housewife.[16] Visually the film also suggests that Henry is at a disadvantage *vis-à-vis* his 'rivals' in love (men who would in reality have been in supremely vulnerable positions, entirely dependent upon the King's whim for their continued survival). Both Peynell (the fictitious suitor to Anne of Cleves)[17] and Culpeper (Catherine Howard's lover) are played by more conventionally handsome actors in the matinée idol tradition, the former by John Loder, the latter by Robert Donat. Thus Laughton's lugubrious-looking Henry is tacitly positioned as the underdog in love, and his suits are given an indulgent, comic treatment, whereas theirs are presented in full earnest. The comic filter through which the marital politics of the reign is read thus nullifies the national political situation, the pressures of confessional conflict and popular unrest, and strips Henry of most of the power which made him so terrifying, while (in a classic tyrannical manoeuvre) displacing responsibility for their fate upon his wives and ministers.

Kulik notes the implied paradox that, 'Although Korda's Henry is tender and sentimental as well as blustering and vulgar, the emphasis is always on Henry as "victim" of manipulating women.'[18] On closer inspection, the apparent contradiction between the sentimentality, the bluster and the victimhood proves to be part of the same childish character type, those facets of the stereotypical sexually innocent hero that characterised British 'romantic' comedy.

The infantilisation of Henry that the film effects is something that critics and reviewers have frequently remarked upon, albeit without always recognising that it is a central element in the film's narrative strategy. The *New York Times* reviewer, for example, noted the simplicity and openness of the performance, while, more recently, Sarah Street has remarked on the 'childlike sympathy and humour' with which Laughton plays the role. Simon Callow, noting Laughton's tendency towards emphasising 'babyish' qualities in his previous roles, detected a variation on this theme in his portrayal of Henry's gait, which suggests, to Callow's actorly eye, the deportment of a toddler ('with all the velocity of a newly initiated walker, he hurls himself across rooms, snatching at people and things along the way').[19] This shrewd observation draws out a crucial element in the captivating idiosyncrasy of Laughton's performance in the early scenes. The audacity with which he approaches the role is captivating, and a good deal of that captivation, and the undoubted 'danger' which he creates, lies in the audience's astonishment at the literal and dramatic momentum he brings to the role, and the concomitant implication that at any moment he might, again quite literally, fall flat on his face (as when he propels himself through the hall towards the chapel, stopping only to beckon to Jane Seymour, and then almost drags her off her feet in his impatience to be married). This is high-wire acting of the highest order. But this infantile quality to the King goes much further than the accidents of gait and manner, and goes to the substance of the film itself.

It is surely no accident that Korda, who maintained a lifelong interest in the psychological aspects of cinema, and one of whose earliest silent features was apparently a treatment of Sigmund Freud's *Interpretation of Dreams*, should have chosen to interpret Henry's marital history in such an obviously cod-Freudian way.[20] The fact that, for example, Henry is sexually aggressive (albeit fumbling and ultimately ineffective) in Catherine Howard's bedroom, but naive, outmanoeuvred and always finally impotent in his own, suggests most clearly that the model of sexuality through which the role is interpreted is that of the adolescent boy (even, perhaps, the pre-Oedipal infant, the stage of orality and unlimited but unfocused desires), rather than the adult male. The adolescent boy, like his older, equally stereotypical, equivalent and successor, the henpecked husband (significantly the other role that Henry plays in the course of the film), is not in control of his own domestic space. He occupies it on sufferance under the authority of a dominant woman: in the case of the boy she is the mother, in that of the husband, the shrewish wife.[21] Hence the crucial importance afforded within *Henry VIII*'s domestic politics to the role of the King's Nurse, who, quite ahistorically, controls the royal bedchamber and does everything else but tuck the King up at night (a task she nevertheless performs symbolically by preparing the bed prior to his retiring on three separate occasions).

The representation of the Nurse as Henry's surrogate mother is stressed in a number of key scenes. On her first appearance her control of the bedchamber is signalled by her role as 'tour guide' and provider of prurient information about the King's nocturnal activities for the 'excited' ladies-in-waiting. This control is reasserted in her next scene as she routs the pompous Chamberlain, Cornell (played by Claud Allister: a version of the Tudor Chief Gentleman of the Privy Chamber who controlled access to the King's private apartments), with a mixture of acerbic wit ('CORNELL: What do you suppose I've been doing for the past hour? / NURSE: Swallowing the poker by the look of you') and the assertion of her prior claim to the right to attend to Henry's bodily needs ('Fool, would *I* harm the King, who nursed him from his birth?').[22] Having established her credentials, the remainder of the scene – and, indeed, of her role in the film – is dedicated to confirming that this particular mother does indeed know best, and that the King can do nothing effective for himself without her approval and assistance. Having placed her 'magic charm' beneath the royal pillow to ensure the conception of a son and heir, she confidently declares, 'Now you'll see, it'll be a boy!' (a line added later to the original screenplay). The next shot vindicates her confidence by fading up over the sound of a baby crying to a view of a line of smiling male courtiers (symbolic of the satisfied political nation) and a pan to the Nurse holding the new Prince of Wales.

That the nursery remains the Nurse's realm – and that the whole palace is effectively part of the nursery – is confirmed in the subsequent scenes in which she chides Henry for upsetting the baby. In the first she silences him as he approaches the cradle with a wave of her hand, and finally shoos him from the room ('Ooh, no, no, no, no, no! Get off; you and your nonsense – no great big beard in the child's face. You'll frighten him out of his wits' – another added line). In the second, set in the gardens at Hampton Court, she waylays him as he strides along, proudly displaying his son to the ladies of the court, and brusquely punctures his *amour propre*:

NURSE: A pretty thing – to hold the child hatless in the blazing sun! [*To the baby*] There, Lovely, come to one who loves you! [*To Henry*] Have you lost your wits to treat him so?

HENRY (*like a naughty child*): Why, I never thought ...

NURSE: You never *thought*! What are brains for but to think with? But no – you must strut among your light(s) o' love, while my poor babe roasts in your arms.

HENRY: *Your* poor babe(?) *My son!*

NURSE: *Your Son?* My *CHARM!*[23]

The final line, which undercuts Henry's central claim to masculine potency (his capacity to sire a son), leaving him confounded and embarrassed as the ladies drift away, signals the King's reduction to adolescent status in these early scenes; and makes clear the reasons for the particularly coy treatment of the bedroom scenes in a film ostensibly concerned with the sexual life of England's most married monarch.

Henry's role as comic, ineffectual lover in these scenes is prepared for in the previous shots of his 'stealing off to Catherine's room with the greatest secrecy and unexpectedly coming upon a sentry' – indeed, a whole series of sentries who 'instantly turn ... out the Guard, as in duty bound'. The comedy of the scene, reliant on the association of Henry with a schoolboy sneaking off to his girlfriend's room, hoping that the adults will not catch him, further emphasises his infantilised lack of authority in his own court. (That even in Catherine's bedroom Henry is never really sexually threatening is suggested in this brief exchange between King and future wife: 'HENRY: Still afraid of me, Kate? / CATHERINE: Of you? No. / HENRY: Of whom, then? / CATHERINE: Of – myself – perhaps.' That it is Henry who is potentially cowed by her is demonstrated when he asks her, 'What would you say if I were not the King?' Her swift response, 'Get out of my room!', confounds

12. *The ailing King is put to bed by Culpeper (Robert Donat).*

him, until she offers the comforting coda, 'That's what I would say, if you were not the King. But since you are, I expect the King's commands.')[24] And this transcription of modern comic codes on to Tudor history goes further, as the heavily populated bedchambers of the central characters, which in reality would have been staffed by the gentlemen and grooms, or ladies and maids of the King and Queen's privy chamber, are replaced by the single-occupancy bedrooms of modern suburban houses in which individuals might plausibly meet for clandestine trysts. So, for the purposes of the film, the ageing King of England becomes the bashful adolescent suitor of countless conventional comedies.

For the conventional fictional bourgeois adolescent, whose early experiences with girls traditionally take place in spaces beyond his control, his own bed provides a retreat from, rather than the focus for sexual competition, with its associations of humiliation at the hands of older girls and rival boys. It offers the prospect of comfort and security (most notably during periods of illness). Hence it is significant that in *Henry VIII* we see Henry in his own bed only twice, and on each occasion he is seeking comfort rather than sexual satisfaction, once when he is exhausted and ill after having unwisely challenged a younger man to a wrestling match, once sitting on the marital bed in the card-playing

scene with Anne of Cleves.[25] The association of the former scene with
notions of safety and maternal nurture is evident in the way that Culpeper tenderly tucks the King beneath the blankets. But the second scene,
despite initial appearances, also conforms to the same pattern, presenting
Henry as the innocent child out of his depth in the company of a cunning
woman.

Ostensibly, the presentation of Anne of Cleves (memorably played
with a comic German accent by Elsa Lanchester) and her dialogue with
Henry in the bedchamber scene position her as the (literal) innocent
abroad, naive about sex and unwilling to give herself up to the King's
advances. It is Henry who has to deliver a short lesson on 'the birds and
the bees' for his wife's benefit.

> HENRY: (Did your mother not talk to you about ... ?) All that stuff
> about children being found under gooseberry bushes – that's not
> true.
> ANNE: Oh, no – it was der shtork.
> HENRY: The stork?
> ANNE: Der shtork flies in der air mit der babes und down der chimney
> drops.
> HENRY: Er – no, Madam, that isn't true either. When a hen lays an egg,
> it's not entirely all her own doing.
> ANNE: You mean, sometimes it vas der cuckoo?
> HENRY (*giving it up*): Yes – it was the cuckoo.[26]

Both the sub-text and the inter-text of the scene tell a different and
more compelling story, however. Anne's pose as the sexual ingénue is,
as the earlier sequences set in Cleves reveal, just that: a pose. She is
actually already committed, emotionally and sexually, to Peynell, whom
Henry had sent as ambassador to her brother ('to watch over Holbein'),
but who fell for Anne himself instead. Whether or not Anne and Peynell
are lovers in the sexual sense when we first encounter them in a field of
splendidly unconvincing sunflowers (in *Cleves?*) is coyly left unsaid. But
the wryly risqué dialogue and 'business' combine to suggest that they
are.

> PEYNELL: As you will, Princess.
> ANNE: And why 'Princess'? (*Softly*) Last night you called me 'Anne'.
> PEYNELL: [*Looking meaningfully into the middle-distance*] Last night I –
> forgot *everything*. To-day ...
> ANNE: *To-day* – forget everything but last night![27]

In the following sequence, an innuendo worthy of the *Carry On* films underlines the suggestion of a sexual relationship between the two. In painfully unconvincing broken English (worse even than Lanchester's), the Duke of Cleves (in reality Anne's brother, but cast here seemingly as her father, and played by William Austin) announces to Holbein (John Turnbull) that he will fetch Anne, with the memorable phrase, 'I will make it that she came already'. There is then a quick cut to a shot of Anne holding a plucked flower in her hands while looking admiringly up at Peynell. That the future queen has been deflowered, and is consequently more knowledgeable about sexual matters than she suggests to Henry, is thus economically suggested to the audience prior to her arrival in England. Her aim in the subsequent bedroom scene with Henry is, as the preparatory business makes clear, to make herself as repellent to him as possible in order to persuade him to grant her a divorce, allowing her to be with Peynell instead.

Henry's ostensible role as sexual predator is thus ironically undercut by the audience's prior knowledge of, and sympathy with, Anne's character and predicament. But other elements of the scene reinforce that effect. Lanchester, for whom the role of Anne was written, brought to the part a readily identifiable 'star quality' and a history of playing 'experienced' women and comic characters in other films, that was already working against her role as a straightforward ingénue. For British audiences there was an additional sexual resonance to her 'star' persona, a product of her role as a founder (when still in her late teens and fresh from the Isadora Duncan academy) of the avant garde London theatre and revue club, 'The Cave of Harmony'. There she had developed an act that effectively combined her childlike appearance and figure with a reputation for a Bohemian lifestyle and sensibility. A deft portrayer of faux innocence, she would perform comic Cockney songs and sentimental Victorian children's ballads ('I Danced with a Man, Who Danced with a Girl, Who Danced with the Prince of Wales', and 'Please Sell no More Drink to My Father') with an ironic knowingness that struck contemporaries as both dangerously funny and sexually provocative. As Anthony Le Touzel put it, 'occasionally she said shocking things in the usual Bohemian manner, but always so naively that there was no shock left in them, and they were merely humorous'. 'In those days Elsa possessed a quality of fascination that was entirely and exclusively her own. She is the very essence of sex-appeal and violent femininity, without being coy or clinging.'[28] That Laughton and Lanchester were husband and wife added further levels of 'knowingness' to the dynamics of the

13. 'No sex, please ... ': Henry and Anne of Cleves (Elsa Lanchester).

scene. The camerawork, allowing the occasional 'exposure' of her more
glamorous side, before she remembers herself and restores her comic
'gargoyle' pose for Henry's benefit, also underscores the reversal of the
scene's ostensible dynamic and puts Anne effectively 'on top'. Henry is
reduced to the status of the schoolboy out of his depth in the bedroom
of the older, more experienced girl.

The royal bedroom is thus presented as an arena for broad comedy,
and the new queen is represented not as vulnerable (both sexually and
politically) in a private space (and realm) wholly dominated by male
values and agenda that are foreign to her, but as herself in command,
and more than capable of negotiating her way out of the situation, if
necessary by threatening the King.

ANNE: Don't shout!
HENRY: I'm not shouting!
ANNE: You *are*!
HENRY: W-w-what am I going to do with you?
ANNE: Chop my head?
HENRY: Probably.
ANNE: You daren't.
HENRY: Why not?

ANNE: Because in Europe I vill make such a scandal as you neffer
heard! It is not der first time that you chop the head. Henry der vife
butcher, that's what they shall call you!

HENRY: I don't care what you say. I'm not going to live with you.[29]

Henry's defeat by Anne here is the prelude to the longer-term sub-
jection to scheming women that characterises the rest of the film. From
this point onwards the Nurse disappears from the action, and the King's
disillusioning marriage to Catherine Howard marks in brief space his
switch from young innocent to deluded old cuckold, and finally to
henpecked husband in his marriage to Catherine Parr. In each case Henry
is subjected to the agitated, excessive, 'nagging' talk of women, a form
of speech that becomes so insistent that it exceeds the margins of the
scenes and continues unabated in the black frames between shots.

The final sequence of the film leaves the audience with an image of
the frail, impotent Henry, trapped in his fireside chair, forced to endure
the unceasing tirade of his last wife's nagging. Her speech (much expanded from the original screenplay) begins before the first shot of the
scene, and does not end until she has left the room: '(No, Henry, you're
an easy-going man, always getting yourself into trouble, and *who* has to
suffer, I should like to know …) I don't know what I'm going to do
with you (I'm sure, what with one thing and another, my life isn't worth
living … ').[30] Henry is given the final word, as he occupies the screen
alone, but only to signal his resigned acceptance of defeat. Standing
beneath the royal coat of arms, with the motto *'Dieu et mon droit'*
conspicuously displayed, Henry utters the epigrammatic summation,
'Six wives – and the best of them's the worst.'[31]

This manipulation of stereotypes (the nagging wife, the innocent
adolescent male, the henpecked husband) that accommodates the particular details of Henry's history into a wider, universal, 'international'
experience is, of course, the hallmark of Korda's approach to national,
historical themes. He had employed precisely the same motifs and situations in his earlier (silent) historical film, *The Private Life of Helen of
Troy* (made in Hollywood in 1927, and based on a novel by John Erskine),
and was to do so again in *The Private Life of Don Juan* and *The Scarlet
Pimpernel* (both 1934), and with variations in the abortive *I, Claudius*
project (1937) and *The Rise of Catherine the Great* (1934).

In *Helen of Troy*, the betrayed husband, Menelaus, is played by Lewis
Stone as a hapless victim of a powerful, sexually aggressive woman:
Helen (played, as we have seen, with nice irony, by Korda's own first

wife, Maria Corda). Stone's Menelaus is a willing cuckold, happy to see Helen taken off to Troy, and only reluctantly persuaded to go to war to seek her return. The final scene presents him, like Laughton's Henry, subjected once more to a familiar pattern of defeat and humiliation. After a brief false triumph, in which it seems that Helen might have been satisfactorily 'domesticated' at last (she asks a maid to bring her some housework), she returns to her former habits on the arrival of the young, virile Prince of Ithaca (played by William Elliott), whom she takes off to her bedchamber in full view of her miserable husband. Rather than attempting to assert his claims as husband and lord of the house, however, Stone's Menelaus decides to accept the inevitability of defeat and withdraws with as much dignity as he can muster to pursue that archetypal American male activity, a fishing trip, leaving Helen in command of the marital bed and in the company of the preferred younger man.[32]

Such images of humiliated, impotent manhood occur throughout Korda's films of this period, most notably in the role of Claudius that caused such difficulties for Laughton (a character summed up with brutal economy by Michael Korda as 'a stammering fool, and clumsy cripple, and a man who is innocent about women, cuckolded and sexually inept in the eyes of his wife and court')[33] but also in the Scarlet Pimpernel's alter ego, Sir Percy Blakeney, whose marital troubles at home provide an insistent sub-plot to his acts of homosocial derring-do in France ('When I married him, he was a man, he was my lover … and now … [*sighs*]', laments Merle Oberon's Lady Blakeney, a picture of sexual longing and frustration), and still more strikingly in his treatment of that great icon of predatory male sexuality, Don Juan.

Korda's *The Private Life of Don Juan* (initially given the revealing title *Exit, Don Juan*) is, characteristically, a study of male sexual failure as well as an interesting meditation on the cult of celebrity (everyone prefers the myth of the great lover to the reality). His protagonist (played by Douglas Fairbanks Senior) is presented in middle age, returning home from his conquests to find his name and reputation usurped by a young impostor. The latter is finally killed off, somewhat conveniently, by a jealous husband, and Don Juan, encouraged by his steward Leporello (Melville Cooper), decides to go into retirement in a country inn. After six months, however, he tires of the good life of wine, cooked breakfasts and song, and tries to resume his balcony-leaping, philandering career. The reviews are, however, far from encouraging (one young belle tells him, 'You look and speak just like my dear father did … he would have been just about your age now'), and the only serious offer he receives is a less than flattering proposal of marriage from his aged landlady (beginning, 'You've no money, no looks, and very little brain'). As a final, despairing gamble he returns to the scene of his former triumphs in Seville, only to find that everyone prefers the legend of the 'dead' lover to the living reality. His failure to live up to his own reputation ('My dear husband was so much bigger, and broader, and far better looking,' declares his wife Dona Dolores [Benita Hume]), leads to his being denounced as an impostor, and finally to humiliation at the hands of his shrewd spouse. Only once he has been reduced to a thoroughly 'domesticated' figure, resigned to staying faithful to the one woman who still wants him, are 'normal' marital relations resumed.[34]

When Korda turned to a female subject in *The Rise of Catherine the Great* (1934, ostensibly directed by Paul Czinner, but in fact very much a Korda creation), the motif of sexual innocence was again applied, and the historical Empress's reputedly voracious sexual appetite was subjected to the same drastic bowdlerisation as Henry VIII's had been in the previous year. Catherine, whom some writers still maintain died, crushed *in flagrante delicto* with a horse, is repackaged as a chaste, faithful wife (played by Elisabeth Bergner), whose only love is her husband, Tsar Peter (Douglas Fairbanks Junior). It is the latter's philandering that prompts her to invent stories of her own affairs in an attempt to make him jealous and win back his affections.

In each of these films, the heroic subject is rendered sexually innocent, freed of ulterior, or even complex, desires and sexual history, in order to engage with the audience's assumed sympathy for the 'victim' or underdog in any competitive situation. All the troublesome aspects of a mature sexual identity are displaced on to other figures in the films – either the desired object itself (the libidinous Tsar Peter, the vampish Helen or, in *Henry VIII*, the more interesting, complex and ambitious character of Catherine Howard), or peripheral figures such as Empress Elizabeth in *Catherine the Great* ('the most shameless rake who ever wore a petticoat' – played, in an intriguing piece of casting, by Flora Robson).[35] But this sexual squeamishness should not be taken to imply that the films are incapable of any seriousness or moments of mature reflection. As Michael Korda notes, *Henry VIII* in particular is a complex film, generically absorbing a mixture of modes and moods that critics at the time found disconcerting.[36] Although Laughton's Henry enjoys a consistently comic trajectory through the film, moving sublimely from adolescent child to henpecked geriatric without ever really gaining full emotional maturity or self-knowledge (and hence allowing the actor to avoid the full, troubling sexual implications of the role), and without even (except for a brief moment after his 'betrayal' by Catherine Howard) ever knowing real sorrow or pain, those around him inhabit a world that is inherently tragic — and is so because of his actions.

The film leaves little doubt, for example, that Anne Boleyn is innocent of the charges of multiple adultery levelled against her, and for which she will die. The cynical reasons for the condemnation are readily acknowledged early in the film.

> 1ST LADY: Anne Boleyn — was she guilty, do you think?
>
> 2ND LADY: All her lovers confessed.
>
> CATHERINE HOWARD: Under torture. I believe she was as innocent as you or I.
>
> 2ND LADY: Thank(s) for the compliment!
>
> 1ST LADY: She died so that the King may be free to marry Lady Jane Seymour.[37]

Both the suffering that this imposes upon Anne and the dignity with which she accepts her fate are absorbed within the film's emotional texture. The pathos of Anne's courage, coupled with her awareness of her own frailty (symbolised by that 'little neck'),[38] give her scenes on the scaffold great power. Yet our sympathy for Anne is never allowed to harden into dislike for, or even resentment of, Henry. Guilt for her death is displaced among the gentlewomen gossiping over her fate, Jane Seymour — obliviously preparing for her own marriage with an inanely beatific grin on her face while Anne is awaiting her death — and the various royal servants (the executioners, the carpenter who is building the scaffold, the crowds who bustle in to watch the execution) who are the instruments of the royal will. While each of their actions seems in bad taste, Henry's boyish eagerness for the gun to be fired to signal that he can marry again seems merely 'natural'. In a neat trick of misdirection, the audience's attention is focused in Henry's scenes on the forthcoming wedding with all its 'healthy' connotations, rather than on the judicial murder that makes it possible. Consequently his 'private life' remains essentially comic, even while everyone about him moves to a more sombre beat.

SIX
Fade-out?

Since Korda's death in January 1956 the reputation of *Henry VIII* has, like Laughton's old King, fallen away considerably. While it remains a much-loved film, and film historians, critics and Korda's biographers have been mindful of its importance, its status as, in Jeffrey Richards's words, an 'epoch-making' film has not been fully reflected in the literature. Significantly, it failed to make the cut in the British Film Institute's list of the 360 'Film Classics' (although the less coherent and ultimately less satisfying *Things to Come* was chosen, and is the subject of an excellent critical appreciation by Christopher Frayling), and its omission is symptomatic.[1] In part it is a reflection of an inherent prejudice against historical films (or, more dismissively, 'costume pictures') in current notions of what constitutes 'classic', canonical cinema. But it is also a function of the apparent aesthetic limitations of the film, and of Korda's own understated directorial technique.

What held Korda back aesthetically (if we accept for a moment that his work was limited in this way) was not so much inherent weakness, but the more mundane issue of the quality of the writing on which he had to rely. Mindful of the need, at least in his early years, to tailor his scripts to what he saw as English tastes, he was frequently forced – as he was with *Henry VIII* – into an over-reliance upon Arthur Wimperis (acting as an English equivalent of the standard Hollywood 'gag-man') to add a leaven of humorous lines to Biró's frequently over-deliberate 'wordy' dialogue. Too often the effect of these 'Wimperisms' was to unbalance the script entirely, turning it into a rather laboured progression from one sub-Wildean *bon mot* or aphorism to another, islands of mannered levity in a sea of more serious material ('CROMWELL: If Your Majesty would but consider it [re-marriage]...' / HENRY: I would consider it – I would consider it the victory of optimism over experience [*general laughter, led by Henry*]'). The results could sometimes be crushingly banal, as when the Second Lady replies to the suggestion that

Anne Boleyn will die so that Henry can marry Jane Seymour, 'Yes, she thinks that's what they mean when they say "chop and change".' (Not even Catherine Howard's 'Don't! It's no jesting matter' can render the line bearable.)[2]

As for the question of directorial technique: Korda was certainly no pioneering innovator in the manner of D. W. Griffith, Eisenstein or Hitchcock. We are not constantly startled by the composition of his shots, or the audacity of his editing. What effects are achieved in the lighting, camerawork and settings of his films (as in the lustrous textures and tones of the monochrome interiors of *Rembrandt*) were, on the face of it, the work of others: of Périnal's subtle, sensuous lighting, Vincent Korda's evocative design and, in the case of *Henry VIII*, Laughton's incandescent performance in the title role. The director, by comparison, seems an almost marginal figure among these prodigious talents, merely the catalyst that allowed the other elements spontaneously to combust. But Korda did more than simply assemble and inspire his team. Although seldom ranked among the great auteurs of European cinema, he did bring a distinct directorial vision to *Henry VIII* and his other great successes of the 1930s. Central to his conception of the role of the director was that ability, identified by both Michael Korda and Paul Tabori, to understand and bring out the best from his actors.[3] For Korda it was the performances that counted, hence, like many of his British contemporaries, he looked to the theatre for the stars who would supplement his stable of London Films regulars and give his films greater box-office potential. But, unlike those contemporaries, he looked not to the musical theatre, the revues or the music hall for his big names, but to the classic theatre of the Old Vic and the Aldwych, bringing in actors of the calibre of Olivier, Ralph Richardson and, as in *Henry VIII*, Laughton. As Richardson later observed, what Korda did, having matched his stars to their roles, was frequently to allow them considerable freedom in which to interpret those roles, and find their own performances.

Korda's sympathy with the idea of the actor as artist rather than disposable property was a function of a sensibility that was, for all his long experience in the film industry, still essentially dramatic in spirit, rooted in theatrical notions of performance and actorly creativity. Having assembled his cast, he saw his role as to inspire them with the spirit of the story they were making together, surround them with the most impressive sets possible, and then let them get on with the business of realising their own performances in relation to each other.[4] Hence the predominance of long- and medium-shots in many of his films of the 1930s, which meant not only (as cynics observed) that he got full value from the sets by showing more of them for more of the time, but also allowed the interaction between the actors that developed naturally on set to be transferred directly to the screen (as opposed to generating it solely via close-ups and reaction shots during the editing process). Hence also the number of his films that, like *Marius* or *Catherine the Great*, originated in stage plays.

Korda can, then, be criticised for not having realised the full potential of the new medium, for remaining 'stage bound' in many of his early British films. But in doing so he brought distinct advantages to his productions. The hybrid of cinematic possibility and theatrical sensibility that is *Henry VIII* is not unlike those early printed books, the incunabula, that retained many of the characteristics of the handwritten manuscripts that preceded them. Like them it adapted form to content, bringing theatrical protocols of rehearsal to the shoot, and thereby allowing Laughton's magisterial performance as the King the room to grow on set in a way that proved impossible in Sternberg's more assertively director-driven regime in the later *I, Claudius*. The result was that, whereas *I, Claudius* remains 'the epic that never was', and the performance that might have been Laughton's masterpiece can be glimpsed only in the fragments of the film that were shot, his Henry was fully realised and remains a monument to his talents. When all the information about low costs and high profits, skilful marketing and overseas sales has been digested, this is probably the film's most convincing claim to greatness.

APPENDIX
The Six (Historical) Wives of Henry VIII

CATHERINE OF ARAGON

Despite her abrupt dismissal in the opening caption of the film (' ... her story is of no particular interest – she was a respectable woman. So Henry divorced her'), Catherine of Aragon was probably the most interesting of Henry's six wives. She was certainly the longest serving and longest suffering. Having been married in 1509, Henry and Catherine were not formally 'divorced' until 1533 (or, rather, their marriage was annulled at that time, on the grounds that, being incestuous – she being the widow of Henry's brother Arthur – it should never have been sanctified in the first place), six years after the King first demanded an annulment and began his relationship with Anne Boleyn. Catherine was an intellectual of some stature (the Dutch scholar Erasmus thought her learning was equal, or even superior, to Henry's own), and a patron of scholars, who ensured that her daughter Mary was educated to the highest European standards. She died, in internal exile, in 1536, only months before Anne Boleyn herself.

The standard biography of Catherine remains Garret Mattingly, *Catherine of Aragon* (London and Boston, 1941). On her scholarship and sponsorship of scholars, see Maria Dowling, 'The Humanist Support for Catherine of Aragon', *Bulletin of the Institute for Historical Research*, No. 56 (1982).

ANNE BOLEYN

Anne Boleyn has proved the most controversial of Henry's wives. At the time Henry's decision to abandon Catherine for Anne polarised the nation. When the 'divorce' campaign led to the break with Rome, the divisions solidified into confessional dogma. Those who favoured the 'old' Catholic faith saw the new queen as 'that whore Nan Boleyn', the slut who seduced Henry from both his wife and the true faith; advocates of the 'new' reformed religion presented her as the godly queen who brought the light of truth to a blind, superstitious land. Historians still differ over the extent of Anne's personal commitment to reformed religion and political influence in the early 1530s. Her reign as queen consort was, however, short lived, lasting little more than the thousand days of popular legend. In May 1536 she was suddenly arrested on charges of multiple adultery with a number of Henry's closest companions, and of incest with her own brother, George, Viscount Rochford. She denied the allegations, as did all of her co-defendants save one, a court musician named Mark Smeaton. Within weeks she was dead, executed like her supposed lovers on Tower Green. Was she guilty as charged? Historians, once again, differ, but have in the main concluded that she was not. But, the obvious question of why, if Henry merely wished to be rid of her so that he could marry Jane Seymour (as is assumed in the film), he invented such wild, incendiary charges against her, is less often addressed. That Anne exerted a powerful sexual attraction, not only to Henry but to many of the men around her at court is clear, however, and that is probably the crucial factor, not only in her rise to prominence, but also in her destruction. Such sexual magnetism, especially when allied to a forceful personality, was a powerfully disruptive force in a court dominated by patriarchal values and the sexual double standard that said that male sexual desire might be acknowledged and freely expressed but assertive female sexuality remained taboo.

In Korda's film we encounter Anne (Merle Oberon) in her chamber in the Tower of London, already condemned and stoically if stylishly awaiting her death. Her innocence is assumed by the majority of her ladies, and, in the absence of any further exploration of her religious beliefs or personal history, the viewer is encouraged simply to admire her beauty and grace under pressure.

The best biography is Eric Ives, *Anne Boleyn* (Oxford, 1986), which makes the case for Anne as an advocate of religious reform, and dismisses the allegations of adultery as politically inspired fabrications. For a more critical view of her religious position, and the suggestion that she may have been guilty of some or all of the crimes alleged against her, see the essays in G. W. Bernard, *Power and Politics in Tudor England* (Aldershot, 2000). For a re-examination of the evidence against her, see Greg Walker, 'Rethinking the Fall of Anne Boleyn', *Historical Journal*, No. 45 (2002).

JANE SEYMOUR

Jane Seymour is probably the queen least well served by Korda's *Henry VIII*. Rather than the vain, vacuous character concerned only with her clothes and appearance represented by Wendy Barrie, the historical Queen Jane was a shrewd player of the political game. Her reputation as a somewhat bland figure is as much the result of her brief reign, and the fact that she followed the volatile Anne Boleyn in Henry's bed (the King declared that he had come out of hell and into heaven with his new marriage) as to anything intrinsic in her character. Her subtle playing of Henry's affections (on one occasion she returned a gift of a purse of coins unopened, telling the messenger that she could accept nothing from the King until God had sent her a good marriage, a gesture that convinced Henry of her virtue and greatly inflamed his passion for her) suggests that she was every bit as capable of looking after herself as her predecessors had been. As the wife who bore him his only legitimate son (she died giving birth to the future Edward VI in 1537), Jane was posthumously assured a prime position in the King's affections. It was alongside her that he asked to be buried when he died in 1547.

In its handling of the Seymour marriage, the film condenses the chronology considerably. Henry did not marry Jane on the day of Anne Boleyn's execution; he merely obtained the special licence to remarry on that day. The couple were actually betrothed on the following day, and were not finally married until 30 May 1536. The opportunity to underscore Henry's ruthless, infantile impatience by compressing the story into a single sequence proved too good for Korda to miss, however, leading to one of the film's most memorable juxtapositions of life and death, as the opening sequence cuts between preparations for Anne's execution in one palace, and for Jane's wedding in another – culminating in Henry's rush for the chapel on hearing the gunshot that announces that Anne's head is off.

Jane Seymour awaits a full scholarly biography, but there is good material in J. J. Scarisbrick, *Henry VIII* (2nd edn, New Haven, 1997).

ANNE OF CLEVES

Anne of Cleves is, with Catherine Howard, the queen given most attention in *Henry VIII*, and is the focus of much of the comedy in the film. While it grossly exaggerates aspects of her character and plays her marriage to Henry for laughs, the film nevertheless captures something of the dynamic of the historical Anne's relationship with Henry. Rather than treat her as the victim of Henry's fickle tastes (the 'poor, plain Anne' of many history books, whom the King did not fancy and cast aside), the film presents her as a woman who skilfully determines her own destiny. In this, it arguably gets things right where many a historian has erred.

The facts of the story are quickly told. Henry, from his first encounter with Anne, was repelled by her appearance, agreeing to marry her only to avoid a diplomatic crisis. On his wedding night, however, his manhood failed him, and Henry emerged the next morning complaining that 'I liked her before not well, but now I like her much worse', and convinced that she was no virgin. He later elaborated that he 'misliked ... her body for the hanging of her breasts and the looseness of her flesh' – features which the pert-breasted, slim virgin of Tudor medical wisdom ought not to have possessed. The problem, such as it was, probably lay with Henry rather than Anne's maidenhood; for contemporary accounts suggest that she, while not beautiful, was certainly no less attractive than any of his other wives. The marriage was, however, never consummated, and Henry sought the earliest opportunity to have it annulled.

What Anne herself made of all this is a question of some interest. It is often suggested that she was indeed, as she presents herself in the film, so naive in sexual matters that she did not realise that anything was wrong. This suggestion is based upon a curious conversation between Anne and her English maids some months after the wedding. When one of the ladies asked if she was with child, Anne replied that she was not. The conversation continued, with the ladies suggesting that Anne could not be certain that she was not, unless she was still a maid (virgin). She then replied, 'How can I be a maid ... and I sleep every night with the King? ... When he comes to bed he kisses me, and takes me by the hand, and bids me "Good night, sweetheart"; and in the morning he kisses me and bids me, "Farewell, darling". Is this not enough?' When Lady Rutland suggested, 'There must be more than this or it will be long ere we have a Duke of York,' Anne is said to have replied, 'Nay, I am contented, I know no more.'

The idea that Anne was really this naive is hard to accept. The kind of sexual innocence that many young women, and even some men, brought to the marriage bed in the Victorian period was much less common in the sixteenth century, especially among aristocratic women of Anne's class whose social role was to produce heirs for their husbands.

And there is evidence that Anne knew very well that something was wrong with Henry's nocturnal performance, because she went to Cromwell with worries about their marriage soon after their wedding night. Cromwell did not record what was said, however, and did nothing – any suggestion of royal impotence was, of course, an explosive political issue. So there matters rested until Henry's attentions turned to the young and vivacious Catherine Howard. It was only then that Anne came out with her 'naive' remarks about her lack of sexual experience with the King. The obvious conclusion is that she, mindful of the fate of her predecessor, and not wishing to share it, was securing her own escape route from the marriage. By playing the innocent, and putting on public record the fact that the marriage was never consummated, she was making it easier for the King to annul their union and move on to Catherine. There would be no need to invent crimes or misdemeanours in order to secure what Shakespeare was to call 'the long divorce of steel'. They could simply negotiate the terms of a settlement, and part. And this, as the film suggests, was what happened, with Anne driving a hard bargain for her agreement. Rather than returning to Cleves (the expected conclusion), she chose to stay in England, with an honourable place at court as the King's 'sister', outliving her erstwhile spouse by some years.

In essence, then, the film is accurate in presenting Anne as a queen who manipulates her own public image in order to escape from a marriage that she does not want (albeit over a period of several months rather than in a single game of cards). In Biró and Wimperis's script, the desire to escape is posited on the ahistorical prior commitment to Peynell, although in fact there is no need to invent reasons why a young woman in her twenties might not wish to be married to a bloated, ill-tempered monarch twice her age. Given that after the annulment Anne lived comfortably on her estates, seemingly untroubled by any male suitors or thoughts of another marriage (a rarity in a culture in which wealthy single women were expected to remarry), it is tempting to wonder whether Anne may not have been more interested in female than male company all along. If this was so (and Anne does make a tempting lesbian icon), the manner in which she secured herself a life with her gentlewomen free from the attentions of both the King and all other potential suitors, does seem all the more skilful.

Two modern biographies of Anne are worth consulting: Mary Saaler, *Anne of Cleves: Fourth Wife of Henry VIII* (London, 1995) is the more accessible; Retha M. Warnicke, *The Marrying of Anne of Cleves: Royal*

Protocol in Tudor England (Cambridge, 2000) rehearses more of the documentary evidence, but is occasionally somewhat wayward in interpreting it.

CATHERINE HOWARD

If Jane Seymour is the queen most obviously undersold by Korda, Biró and Wimperis, Catherine Howard is the chief beneficiary of their generosity. Played as a shrewdly ambitious yet complex character, whose desire for a crown ultimately conflicts with her emotional and sexual commitment to her former lover (Thomas Culpeper), Binnie Barnes's Catherine is probably the film's most consistent and rounded psychological portrait. Historians have been rather less kind, concluding almost without exception that the real Catherine was a young and very foolish woman, who quickly got out of her depth in the world of the court and its politics, unaware of the responsibilities that marriage to the King brought with it. Already sexually experienced when she met and captivated Henry, she seems to have given little thought to what might happen if her sexual history became public knowledge. Still more unwisely, she resumed an affair with one of her former lovers, Culpeper, disregarding that same double standard that brought about the fall of Anne Boleyn: sexual infidelity in a king was only to be expected, but in a queen was high treason. It was only a matter of time before gossip about Catherine's clandestine liaisons with Culpeper leaked out, and Henry had to be told. The scene in the film in which his councillors finally summon the courage to tell him, and he breaks down in tears, is a fairly faithful re-creation of historical events and the King's reaction to them.

The most substantial (and in many ways the most critical) study of Catherine's life and brief reign, is still Lacey Baldwin Smith, *A Tudor Tragedy: The Life and Times of Catherine Howard* (London, 1961).

CATHERINE PARR

Catherine Parr is another woman short-changed by Korda and his writers' stereotypical conception of Henry's wives. Like Catherine of Aragon she was an intellectual, and an author in her own right, having composed a number of Protestant-inflected spiritual works including *The Lamentation of a Sinner*. Far from being the kind of shrew portrayed by Everley Gregg, the historical Catherine was by all accounts a mild-tempered woman, able to sooth Henry through his final illness and raise his spirits during his not infrequent bouts of depression. Rather than nagging him about his health, her strategy was to engage him in theological discussion – a subject close to her own and the King's heart. Her Catholic enemies accused her of seeking to convert Henry to Lutheran heresy (and there may have been some truth in the charge), but, forewarned of their plot, she persuaded the King that she spoke of religious matters only to distract him from his illnesses, and won a reprieve.

Susan E. James, *Kateryn Parr: The Making of a Queen* (Aldershot, 1999) is an excellent study of Catherine's life and beliefs.

There are many single-volume studies covering Henry and all his marriages, of which the best known is probably Antonia Fraser, *The Six Wives of Henry VIII* (London, 1992). Perhaps the liveliest is Karen Lindsay, *Divorced, Beheaded, Survived: A Feminist Account of the Wives of Henry VIII* (Reading, Massachusetts, 1995) which, despite its title, wears its feminism lightly.

Notes

FOREWORD

1. The quotations are from Richards, *The Age of the Dream Palace*, p. 259; Harper, *Picturing the Past*, p. 9; Street, 'Alexander Korda', pp. 161–79; and Callow, *Laughton*, p. 61, respectively.

1. ORIGINS

1. Korda, quoted from a BBC interview, in Kulik, *Korda*, p. 86. This 'authorised version' of the genesis of the project as a battle against the odds is also outlined in Ernest Betts's introduction to the filmscript, published in 1934. 'Everyone thought that Mr Korda was mad,' he concluded succinctly (Betts [ed.], *The Private Life of Henry VIII* [hereafter *Private Life*], pp. xv–xvi). The suggestion is supported by the observation in *Film Weekly* that 'costume pictures, whether grave or gay, are not favoured by the film trade' ('Making British Films for the World', *Film Weekly*, 25 August 1933, pp. 4–5, p. 5).

2. Balcon, *Michael Balcon Presents*, p. 93; Kulik, *Korda*, p. 86. Balcon's associate at Gaumont British, C. M. Woolf, and the banker Leopold Sutro were equally unforthcoming (Tabori, *Korda*, p. 126).

3. Wood, *Mr Rank*, p. 61; Low, *The History of the British Film, 1929–1939*, p. 167.

4. For the finances, see Low, *The History of the British Film, 1929–1939*, p. 167. The rewrites are referred to in a letter from Churchill to his wife Clementine of 18 January 1935, printed in Gilbert (ed.), *Winston S. Churchill*, V (2), p. 1033. 'The Royal Husband' was the working title for the project when Watts visited the set in May 1933 (Stephen Watts, 'Filming the King of Many Wives', p. 27). It had been changed to *The Private Life* ... by 17 June, when E. G. Cousins lamented the change, observing, 'I rather suspect the clumsy [new] title is intended as a "publicity tie-up" with *The Private Life of Helen of Troy*' (Cousins, 'On the British Sets', p. 16).

5. Ian Dalrymple, cited in Oakley, *Where We Came In*, p. 135.

6. Lanchester, *Charles Laughton and I*, p. 121; Wood, *Mr Rank*, p. 61; Oakley, *Where We Came In*, p. 121; *Private Life*, p. xvi; Harper, *Picturing the Past*, p. 22; and Dickinson and Street (eds), *Cinema and State*, p. 76. United Artists invested on the strength of the trade show on 17 August (Low, *The History of the British Film, 1929–1939*, p. 168; Stockham, *The Korda Collection*, p. 50; Watts, 'Alexander Korda and the International Film', p. 12). For the revival income, see Wood, *Mr Rank*, p. 62, Kulik, *Korda*, p. 89, and the surviving correspondence

between London Films and Independent Television in the London Film Productions Collection in the BFI archive.

7. Kulik, *Korda*, p. 88; Callow, *Laughton*, p. 62. The *Daily Mail* review is quoted in Tabori, *Korda*, p. 130; the *Sunday Express* and the *Sydney Morning Herald* in Stockham, *The Korda Collection*, p. 54; *Film Weekly*, 25 August 1933, p. 25; *Picturegoer Weekly*, 5 May 1934, p. 4; and see also *Cinema Quarterly*, 2 (1), Autumn 1933, pp. 39–40. Such judgements have retained their validity. In 1952, Alan Wood described the film as 'so celebrated that it is already passing into legend' (Wood, *Mr Rank*, pp. 61–2), and in her exhaustive history of the British cinema, Rachael Low described it as 'phenomenal … a milestone, not only for London Film Productions, but for the British film industry' (Low, *The History of the British Film, 1929–1939*, p. 167). Jeffrey Richards called it 'a film which, if any does, deserves the epithet "epoch-making"' (Richards, *The Age of the Dream Palace*, p. 259). In Karol Kulik's view it is 'one of the most important films in the development of British Cinema' (Kulik, *Korda*, p. 89); in that of Martin Stockham, it is 'an outstanding film', that 'set new standards in the British film industry' (Stockham, *The Korda Collection*, p. 50). Readers of *Film Weekly* voted *Private Life* the second most popular film of 1933. Intriguingly, the most popular film was *Blossom Time* (British International Pictures, 1934), a romanticised account of the life of Schubert, directed by Paul Stein and starring Richard Tauber (Harper, *Picturing the Past*, p. 40).

8. *Private Life*, p. 46.

9. *Film Weekly*, 16 February 1934, p. 31, and 20 October 1933, p. 33; Callow, *Laughton*, p. 61.

10. *Film Weekly*, 30 March 1934, p. 18; Harper, *Picturing the Past*, p. 23; Kulik, *Korda*, p. 119; *Private Life, passim*; Callow, *Laughton*, pp. 63–8; The Internet Movie Data Base (www.uk.imdb.com).

11. BFI Library, Pressbook, 'The Private Life of Henry VIII' [hereafter BFI Pressbook]; (Tabori, *Korda*, pp. 133 and 122).

12. '"It's a Wonderful Source of Energy", says Merle Oberon, playing in London Films productions' "The Private Life of Henry VIII" of Shredded Wheat', *Film Weekly*, 27 April 1934, p. 40; *Film Weekly*, 1 December 1933, p. 69. For the Fairbankses' admiration for Korda's direction, see 'Making British Films for the World', *Film Weekly*, 25 August 1933, p. 4; Tabori, *Korda*, pp. 129–31.

13. Higham, *Charles Laughton*, p. 69; Lejeune, 'The Private Lives of London Films', p. 82. Korda's analogy is quoted in M. Korda, *Charmed Lives*, p. 104, and Stockham, *The Korda Collection*, pp. 22–23.

14. Young (ed.), *The Diaries of Sir Robert Bruce Lockhart*, Vol. I, p. 392; Street, 'Alexander Korda', pp. 161–2. Street also quotes (p. 165) a memorandum from Percy Crump, joint-secretary to the Prudential, written in mid-1938, which warned his associates that Korda's 'engaging personality and charm of manner must be resisted. His financial sense is non-existent, and his promises (even when they are sincere) worthless … Korda is a very dominant man and dangerous to converse with owing to his powers of persuasion.' See also the varying contemporary assessments of Korda's culpability in the 1937 crash quoted in Kulik, *Korda*, pp. 174–6.

15. Street, 'Alexander Korda', p. 162.

16. Lejeune, 'The Private Lives of London Films; Part V', p. 8. The number of books and story-lines for which the rights were bought up ran into hundreds; although, as what follows will suggest, Korda may have had more philanthropic motives for buying up some of the rights he secured. Street's judgement, while more acerbic than Lejeune's, is not entirely out of sympathy with her conclusion: 'In the final analysis, Korda's achievements as a producer probably outweigh his financial ineptitude, but only just' (Street, 'Alexander Korda', p. 177). See Low, *The History of the British Film, 1929–1939*, pp. 228–9, for a more favourable verdict.

17. For this and the account of Korda's early life which follows, see Kulik, *Korda*, pp. 4–75; M. Korda, *Charmed Lives*, pp. 35–96; and Lejeune, 'The Private Lives of London Films', pp. 82–5.

18. See the next chapter for more details.

19. The directors of London Films were J. S. Cerf (an associate of the French Pathé organisation), J. R. Sutro (representing his father, the banker Leopold Sutro), William Brownlow (the future Lord Lurgan), Captain Arthur Carlyne Neville Dixey (Conservative MP for Penrith and Cockermouth, 1923–35), Grossmith (who was chairman of the board), Biró, and Korda himself. Their head office was at 22 Grosvenor Street, Mayfair. Tabori, *Korda*, p. 121; Stockham, *Korda Collection*, pp. 16–19.

2. THE MAKING OF *THE PRIVATE LIFE OF HENRY VIII*

1. Kulik, *Korda*, p. 85; Higham, *Charles Laughton*, p. 66; M. Korda, *Charmed Lives*, p. 73. For the bust story, see Higham, *Charles Laughton*, p. 66; Wood, *Mr Rank*, p. 61; and Stockham, *The Korda Collection*, p. 14. Elsa Lanchester is sceptical of the suggestion, pointing out that the actor's resemblance to the King was obvious and had often been remarked upon in Laughton's circle (Lanchester, *Charles Laughton and I*, p. 120).

2. Eisner, *The Haunted Screen*, p. 140; M. Korda, *Charmed Lives*, pp. 99–101; Kulik, *Korda*, p. 30.

3. Callow, *Laughton*, pp. 64–5. The production was to open in Wells before moving to London, and ran from 7 November to 2 December 1933. It attracted rather less favourable reviews than the film role that premièred in the preceding month.

4. Tabori, *Korda*, p. 125.

5. Kulik, *Korda*, p. 89; Street, *British National Cinema*, p. 36.

6. M. Korda, *Charmed Lives*, p. 99.

7. The relevant films are *Samson und Delila* (Vienna, 1920); *The Private Life of Helen of Troy* (Hollywood, 1927); and *Der Tänzer Meiner Frau* (Berlin, 1925). Korda was later to craft the role of the nymphomaniac adulteress Messalina (in *I, Claudius*) as a vehicle for his soon to be second wife, Merle Oberon. M. Korda, *Charmed Lives*, p. 73; Kulik, *Korda*, pp. 24, 34, 39 and 194.

8. Tabori, *Korda*, pp. 126 and 128. Elsa Lanchester was to recall that 'those were the days when one did the best one could with a piece of string and a drawing-pin' (Lanchester, *Charles Laughton and I*, pp. 120–1). For the crowd scenes, see M. Korda, *Charmed Lives*, p. 101.

9. *Private Life*, p. xvi; M. Korda, *Charmed Lives*, pp. 100–1; Kulik, *Korda*, pp. 87–8. For critical approval of the sets, see, for example, the *New York Times Film Reviews*, 13 November 1933, p. 989 ('it is a remarkably well-produced film, both in the manner of direction, and in the settings and selection of exterior scenes'); Cousins, 'Charles Laughton at Elstree', *Picturegoer Weekly*, 10 June 1933, p. 32 ('Hampton Court, Windsor, and Greenwich are being faithfully reproduced with period furniture, velvet, damask, cloth of gold'); and *Film Weekly*, 16 February 1934, p. 31 ('The reproduction of Tudor England is magnificently done'). For quibbles over the furniture, see Beard, 'Why Get It Wrong?', pp. 124–5.

10. Harper, *Picturing the Past*, p. 22; BFI Pressbook.

11. *Private Life*, pp. 4, 16 and 8. Unless otherwise stated, all quotations from the film are from Betts's edition. Here and elsewhere, the additional lines printed within rounded brackets are spoken in the film but are not in the printed text, while comments in square brackets are my own additional attempts to illuminate the onscreen business.

12. *Private Life*, pp. 40, 61 and 108.

13. See, for example, Wood, *Mr Rank*, p. 62 ('It was not, according to some critics, a particularly good film. But it proved that British films could rival in gloss and polish the Hollywood product'). Freda Bruce Lockhart was more critical (see 'Is he really Alexander the Great?', *Film Pictorial*, 26 October 1935, quoted in Kulik, *Korda*, p. 134). In Karol Kulik's judgement, Korda's early work, including *Henry VIII*, established a pattern of 'weak narratives, facile characterisation, unconvincing dialogue, and over-emphasised production values' which he 'stubbornly clung to' throughout his career. Favouring 'spectacle for spectacle's sake', he directed films that were often 'hollow', lacking in emotion, even 'flatulent' (Kulik, *Korda*, pp. 294 and 243).

14. M. Korda, *Charmed Lives*, p. 103.

15. *Private Life*, pp. 35 and 95.

16. Eaton, *Chinatown*, p. 16.

17. Higham, *Charles Laughton*, p. 66. Elsa Lanchester noted that Laughton 'read every possible book he could get on the subject, and saw innumerable paintings of Henry VIII' (Lanchester, *Charles Laughton and I*, p. 121).

18. Callow, *Laughton*, pp. 61–2. For the 'authentic' Hampton Court sets, see the BFI Pressbook. Korda was to claim, with characteristic bravado, that 'neither funds nor effort was [sic] spared in staging the picture. Not only were several sets duplicated [and] the mammoth halls of Hampton Court built in the studio, but the costumes required many months to prepare and were made from the finest materials … the cost of Laughton's wardrobe alone amounts to more than $2,500.'

19. *New York Times Film Reviews*, 13 November 1933, pp. 988–9. See also Cousins,

'Charles Laughton at Elstree', p. 2; *Film Weekly*, 2 June 1933, p. 27. The publicity material made much of the similarities between the actor and the portrait but stressed the allegedly serendipitous nature of the likeness as the angle most likely to attract press attention ('Charles Laughton raised his own beard to play the role of the King … Curiously enough, it grew of its own accord in the design worn by England's greatest monarch, and required practically no barbering to make Laughton resemble almost identically Henry's famous portrait' [BFI Pressbook]).

20. Lanchester, *Charles Laughton and I*, p. 121.

21. Callow, *Laughton*, p. 62; Higham, *Charles Laughton*, p. 67.

22. The sequence of shots is described in detail in the surviving continuity script, BFI Archive, Lajos Biró Collection, item 3, reel 2: shot 6 and following. The portrait, attributed to the school of Cremona, was once thought to be of Henry VIII's fool, Will Somers, and is listed in Collins Baker, *Catalogue of the Pictures at Hampton Court*, p. 31. I am grateful to my colleague Dr Anne Marie D'Arcy for pursuing the history of this picture for me, and to Alison Heald of the Curator's Department, Historical Royal Palaces, for further valuable information.

23. *Private Life*, pp. 45–6.

24. Cohan uses the term in the context of *Singin' in the Rain*, but it seems equally appropriate to *Henry VIII* (Cohan, 'Case Study', p. 65). For a sensitive exploration of Laughton's responses to his own sexuality, see Callow, *Laughton*, 'coda'.

25. M. Korda, *Charmed Lives*, pp. 100 and 116.

3. KORDA, ENGLISHNESS AND THE 'INTER-NATIONAL FILM'

1. Watts, 'Filming the King of Many Wives', p. 27. For the multilingual phone calls, see 'Making British Films for the World', *Film Weekly*, 25 August 1933, pp. 4–5; for the multinational team that produced *Henry VIII*, see Kulik, *Korda*, pp. 83 and 96–7; Macnab, *J. Arthur Rank*, p. 67. Variations on the 'joke' were still being recycled in the mid-1940s. George Mikes's satirical squib, *How to be an Alien* (1946), parodied the Korda organisation in its chapter, 'How to be a film producer'. The attendant Nicolas Bentley cartoon shows a producer's door bearing a list of patriotically-named companies from 'Anglo-Saxon Pictures Ltd', through 'Heart of England Films' to 'Pictures of Britain Ltd'. At the foot of the list is the legend: 'Managing Director, Sor Ipolyi Podmaniczky (British)' (reprinted in Mikes, *How to be a Brit*, p. 67; many thanks to Professor Tony Kushner for this and the following references).

2. Stockham, *The Korda Collection*, p. 32.

3. Lane, *The Alien Menace*, pp. 74ff. Greene's review is from *The Spectator*, 5 June 1936. Kulik, *Korda*, p. 143.

4. *World Film News*, Vol. 2, No. 6 (September 1937), pp. 18–19, cited in Richards, *The Age of the Dream Palace*, pp. 43–4.

5. For immigration, see Gough-Yates, 'The European Film Maker in Exile', pp. 97–100, xii and 141 and following, and Gough-Yates, 'Jews and Exiles in British Cinema', pp. 517–41, *passim*; for the diatribe, Burnett and Martell, *The Devil's Camera*, cited in Richards, *The Age of the Dream Palace*, p. 55. See also the still more vitriolic and sustained attack on 'the libidinous Jewish influence behind the films' in Ashton, *The Jew at Bay*, esp. Ch. 14, 'The Burden of the Films', pp. 111–16. *The Kine Year Book* for 1934 was to publish a statement from the ACT that it intended 'to check foreign employment if a Britisher is available capable of undertaking the work required by the company' (Low, *The History of the British Film, 1929–1939*, p. 12). The more positive editorial is in *Film Weekly*, 4 May 1934, p. 5.

6. For Morrison's speech, see *Parliamentary Debates (House of Commons): Official Reports*, 5th Series, 328 (4 November 1937), columns 1197–8; for Street's observations, see her *British National Cinema*, p. 61.

7. For this and what follows in the paragraph, see Greenhalgh, *Ephemeral Vistas*, pp. 121–2. For British anxieties, see Taylor, *The Projection of Britain*, pp. 106–7; and Taylor, 'British Official Attitudes Towards Propaganda Abroad', pp. 23–49 and 34–5.

8. As early as 1925, an FO official, J. D. Gregory, had recognised that 'the era when it was possible either to lead opinion in foreign politics by mere authority or tradition, or to ignore it from Olympian heights, has long since vanished' (quoted in Taylor, *The Projection of Britain*, p. 56). See also Greenhalgh, *Ephemeral Vistas*, p. 125.

9. Tallents, *The Projection of England*, p. 11. The elision of Britain into 'England' betrays the wholly Anglo-centric nature of the 'projection' project as it was pursued in the 1920s and '30s.

10. Greenhalgh, *Ephemeral Vistas*, pp. 124, 122 and (for the quotation below) 125.

11. Taylor, *The Projection of Britain*, pp. 101 and 121; Harper, *Picturing the Past*, p. 8.

12. Cited in Richards, *The Age of the Dream Palace*, p. 63.

13. Street, *British National Cinema*, p. 39; Dickinson and Street (eds), *Cinema and State*, pp. 17 and 30; Richards, *The Age of the Dream Palace*, p. 63. In 1930 it was argued: 'It is horrible to think that the British Empire is receiving its education from a place called Hollywood ... The American film is everywhere and is the best advertisement of American trade and commerce' (Taylor, *The Projection of Britain*, p. 121).

14. Dickinson and Street (eds), *Cinema and State*, p. 5.

15. Tallents, *The Projection of England*, p. 11; Richards, *The Age of the Dream Palace*, p. 248.

16. The involvement of private enterprise was a financial necessity. Foreign Office figures for 1929 suggest that the French government was spending some £500,000 annually on cultural propaganda, the Germans £300,000, and the Italians only marginally less. On 16 December 1930 the British Treasury announced that it would release £2,500 per annum for the same purpose (Taylor, *The Projection of Britain*, p. 139).

17. A DOT memorandum noted in 1928, 'such films are likely to be acceptable because they savour more of entertainment and less of propaganda' (G. E. C. Hatton, 'Industrial propaganda and interest films', Department of Overseas Trade memorandum, 14 May 1928, quoted in Taylor, *The Projection of Britain*, pp. 99–100). For the allusion to vermin, see J. Nock, 'A New Dose of British Propaganda', *American Mercury*, 42, December 1937, p. 482 (also quoted in Taylor, *The Projection of Britain*, p. 75).

18. Hatton, memorandum of 9 December 1929, cited in Taylor, *The Projection of Britain*, pp. 99–100.

19. This was a theme to which Baldwin was to return in many notes and speeches (Williamson, *Stanley Baldwin*, pp. 48, 145 and 205; and Hollins, 'The Conservative Party and Film Propaganda', p. 359).

20. There were reportedly 903 million visits to the cinema made in 1934 alone (see Sedgwick, 'Cinema-going Preferences', p. 2). Despite their reactionary image, it was the Tories who were quickest to react, deploying cinema 'projection vans' to tour working-class districts showing party propaganda, and establishing the Conservative and Unionist Film Association in May 1930 to encourage the production by the mainstream cinema industry of films of a 'patriotic and national character' (see Hollins, 'The Conservative Party and Film Propaganda', pp. 361–8).

21. *Private Life*, p. xvi. Hall's remark was made in a speech to the London Publicity Club in November 1934, quoted in Taylor, *The Projection of Britain*, p. 116. The British Ambassador to Sweden agreed. He remembered the film as 'first class'; albeit, he conceded to the British Legation in Stockholm, 'I have a certain delight in strong and Rabelasian meats' (Harper, *Picturing the Past*, p. 16). For intervention in Peru, see ibid.

22. *Daily Telegraph*, 20 November 1933, cited in Harper, *Picturing the Past*, p. 16.

23. Harper, *Picturing the Past*, p. 9. For the Historical Association resolution, see ibid., p. 66.

24. Quoted in Street, 'Stepping Westward', p. 62, footnote 27.

25. Cole, 'Henry VIII Blacks a Few Critical Eyes', p. 11. Beard, 'Why Get It Wrong?', pp. 124–5.

26. The story is related in Tabori, *Korda*, p. 131. The book in question is Francis Hackett, *Henry the Eighth* (London, 1929).

27. Lindsay, 'The Camera Turns to History', pp. 10–11. A copy of Lindsay's letter of appointment from Korda (he was retained on a fee of £150, payable in instalments) is in the London Film Productions Collection in the BFI archive (LFP Collection C/1069/1) as are copies of the rather more formal contracts for a number of later collaborations (LFP Collection C/1069/2 and C/1069/3).

28. Kulik, *Korda*, p. 10.

29. Basil Wright's description is taken from an interview with Karol Kulik quoted in Kulik, *Korda*, p. 106. For the other quotations, see Lejeune, 'The Private Lives of London Films', p. 83; Wood, *Mr Rank*, p. 62; 'Making British Films for the World', *Film Weekly*, 25 August 1933, p. 4. For the ambivalence sur-

rounding assimilation and cultural conceptions of 'good' and 'bad' Jewish identity in Britain in this period, see a number of the essays in Kushner and Lunn (eds), *Traditions of Intolerance*, esp. Cheyette, 'Jewish Stereotyping and English Literature 1875–1920'.

30. For this and what follows, see Kulik, *Korda*, pp. 19–20, 29–31 and 75; M. Korda, *Charmed Lives*, pp. 15–16, 71 and 86.

31. Gough-Yates, 'The European Film Maker in Exile', pp. 97–100; Tabori, *Korda*, p. 131; M. Korda, *Charmed Lives*, pp. 105–6. On 25 August 1934 Churchill mentioned to his wife, Clementine, that he had reached an agreement with Korda for a contract with London Films for a number of factual short films on subjects of his own choosing. A draft press release drawn up by Churchill on 12 September suggested that the topics covered would include 'Will monarchies return?', 'The rise of Japan', 'Marriage laws and customs', 'Unemployment' and 'Gold'. It also declared that 'Mr Randolph Churchill (Mr Winston Churchill's son) had also been engaged by London Films to assist in the making of the series' (Gilbert [ed.], *Winston S. Churchill*, V (2), pp. 856 and 869). In a letter to Korda of 24 September, Churchill confirmed the further agreement reached over lunch that day for Churchill to produce the scenario for a film on the reign of George V. Churchill was to receive 25 per cent of the net profits, with an advance of £2,500 payable on 1 January 1935, a further £2,500 on completion of the film, and £5,000 'on the day of presentation' (ibid., pp. 876–7).

32. For a useful introduction to the die-hards' position on race, see Cesarani, 'Joynson-Hicks and the Racial Right', pp. 118–39.

33. Watts, 'Alexander Korda and the International Film', pp. 13 and 14–15; 'Making British Films for the World', *Film Weekly*, 25 August 1933, p. 4; Kulik, *Korda*, p. 97.

34. A. Korda, 'Costume Films Have Brought New Life to the Screen', p. 19.

35. Kulik, *Korda*, p. 97; Tabori, *Korda*, p. 204.

36. Kulik, *Korda*, p. 300.

37. For Kerr, see *Out of the Hitler Time*, his daughter Judith's three-volume autobiographical novel (London, 1995), pp. 247–50. Kulik quotes Basil Wright as saying: 'What really happened was, presumably, that Moholy Nagy needed money, and Korda found the means of giving him some' (Kulik, *Korda*, p. 149). For Roberts, see Tabori, *Korda*, p. 136. Gough-Yates, 'Jews and Exiles in British Cinema', p. 535; Korda, *Charmed Lives*, p. 347; Stockham, *The Korda Collection*, p. 25. Marcus is quoted in Gough-Yates, 'Jews and Exiles in British Cinema', p. 535. Thanks to Chris Parker for the Kerr reference.

4. KORDA AND THE POLITICS OF REPRESENTATION

1. Vasudevan, 'The Politics of Cultural Address', p. 151.

2. For female audiences, see *Film Weekly* (30 November 1935) and Harper, *Picturing the Past*, p. 57. For an aversion to 'dry' history, see Harper, *Picturing the Past*, p. 24. Reviewers took a similar line; see *Evening News*, 4 November 1933; *Film Weekly*, 30 November 1935; and the clear declaration in the *Daily Mirror*

of 27 November 1935, 'As to films with facts in them (like fish with bones in it) we try to like them. We don't always succeed' (Harper, *Picturing the Past*, p. 56). For the quotation from Korda, see ibid., p. 21.

3. For the savages, see *Private Life*, p. 88; for the daughters, ibid., p. 49.

4. Harper, *Picturing the Past*, pp. 20–3 and 38; Street, *British National Cinema*, p. 40.

5. Gaines, 'Dream/factory', p. 101.

6. *Private Life*, pp. 42–4.

7. On the 'domestication' of Henry, see Street, *British National Cinema*, p. 40. In a scene ultimately cut from the film, the henpecked husband in the audience at Anne Boleyn's execution is allowed to contemplate wistfully the special freedoms that the King possesses in the area of marital politics. 'Wife: Is it true that the King marries Jane Seymour tomorrow? / Husband: To-day, they say. / Wife: To-*day*? / Husband: Yes (*Enviously*) What it is to be the King. / (*The Wife looks at him with wifely resentment*)' (*Private Life*, p. 8). The removal of this exchange serves to increase the sense of affinity between Henry and henpecked husbands everywhere that is the film's final message.

8. Caption 1: 'Henry VIII had six wives. Catherine of Aragon was the first; but her story is of no particular interest – she was a respectable woman. So Henry divorced her.' Caption 2: 'He then married Anne Boleyn. This marriage also was a failure, but not for the same reason' (*Private Life*, p. 1).

9. Ibid., p. 2.

10. The chirpy royal barber provides an example of the modernising impulse at its most obvious. His small talk and gestures are drawn directly from the enduring stereotype of the English hairdresser's salon: 'You're keeping your hair very well, your Grace'; 'Lovely weather for the time of year, your Grace' (*Private Life*, pp. 41 and 75). Short of asking if the King needed 'something for the weekend', it is hard to think of a feature of the comic barber's repertoire that the character omits.

11. The description of the original event in Wriothesley's *Chronicle* lists the witnesses as 'the Lord Chancellor of England, the Duke of Richmond [Henry VIII's illegitimate son by his lover Elizabeth Blount], [the] Duke of Suffolk, with most of the King's Council, [such] as earls, lords, and nobles of this realm … also the Mayor of London, with the aldermen and sheriffs and certain of the best crafts of London' (Hamilton [ed.], *A Chronicle of England*, I, p. 41). The recent claim by one historian that 'hundreds of ordinary Londoners were there' (Ives, *Anne Boleyn*, p. 409) is thus somewhat misleading.

12. *Private Life*, pp. 4 and 8.

13. Ibid., p. 36. See also the scene between Henry and Culpeper in which the dynamic is reversed and the former offers the latter the benefit of *his* experience on the matter of marriage. 'Thomas, if you want to be happy, marry a woman like my sweet little Jane. Marry a *stupid* woman!' (ibid., p. 20). For what follows, see ibid., pp. 41, 43 and 76.

14. Harper, *Picturing the Past*, pp. 22 and 28; Richards, *The Age of the Dream Palace*, p. 266; *Private Life*, p. 76.

15. *Private Life*, pp. 68 and 77.

16. Street, *British National Cinema*, p. 40.

17. *Private Life*, p. 6. Calais was in fact an English possession until the reign of Mary Tudor. For the following quotations, see ibid., pp. 6–7.

18. See Stevenson, 'The Politics of Violence', p. 147.

19. See *Private Life*, p. 14, for a substantially different version of this sequence.

20. Ibid., p. 95. Note the implicit appeal to US interests and agenda here. See also *Private Life*, p. 102: 'Culpeper: Catherine! Why is there a Council tonight? / Catherine: The French and Germans again, I suppose.' While it acknowledges the costs of such peacemaking from strength ('Henry: A strong fort at Dover, a strong Fleet in the Channel, and we can laugh in their faces. But the money – the money – we must have the money' [*Private Life*, pp. 16–17 and p. 46]), the film ultimately glosses over the economic sacrifices it would necessarily entail. Cromwell's cautious retort to Henry's demand ('New Taxes, sir?' / Henry: New Taxes? My people are bled white already. Yet a way must be found – *must* be found') was cut from the final version.

21. Addison, 'Patriotism Under Pressure', p. 196; Williamson, *Stanley Baldwin*, p. 47. For the quotations below, see ibid., pp. 300–2, and Thompson, *The Anti-Appeasers*, p. 27.

22. Williamson, *Stanley Baldwin*, pp. 47–8; Gilbert (ed.), *Winston S. Churchill*, V, p. 492.

23. Ball (ed.), *Parliament and Politics*, pp. 248 and 271; Lamb, *The Drift to War*, p. 77; Addison, 'Patriotism Under Pressure', p. 196.

24. Gilbert (ed.), *Winston S. Churchill*, V, p. 445.

25. Ibid., p. 450.

26. Ibid., pp. 456–8. On 5 September 1933, Lord Hailsham told the Cabinet that 'Our ports were almost undefended, and our anti-aircraft defence were totally inadequate … Everyone must agree that some increase in expenditure and armaments would be required in the next few years' (ibid., pp. 489–90).

27. Cuthbert Headlam recorded in his diary Dixey's 'highly jubilant' behaviour in the House of Commons smoking room in response to Baldwin's defeat in a division on 22 December 1927 (Ball [ed.], *Parliament and Politics*, p. 138). Churchill's dismissive observation was made in a letter to his wife, Clementine, of 8 March 1935. Dixey was the only Tory MP willing to share a platform with Randolph Churchill who was standing as a maverick die-hard against the government candidate in the Norwood by-election. 'Randolph's foray at Norwood goes very much as I apprehended,' wrote Churchill, gloomily. 'The India Defence League refused to give him any support, and only one Conservative member (and he a crack pot) has appeared on his platform' (Gilbert [ed.], *Winston S. Churchill*, V [2], p. 1105). Dixey was to retire from Parliament in October 1935, thoroughly disenchanted with the policies of the National Government.

28. Kulik, *Korda*, pp. 161 and 252.

29. For the American tours, see Gilbert (ed.) *Winston S. Churchill*, V, pp. 334–5, 345–51 and 418–27. The success of Korda's wooing of Churchill can be judged

from the latter's comments to his wife, Clementine, during January 1935. 'I have great confidence in this man [Korda], and in his flair,' he announced after they had met to discuss the jubilee project. 'Korda certainly gives me the feeling of a genius at this kind of thing' (ibid., V [2], p. 1032).

30. Ibid., pp. 1032–3.

31. For the former suggestion, see Tabori, *Korda*, p. 170; for the latter, ibid., p. 118.

32. Kulik notes, without further reference, that 'there had apparently been minor intrigues perpetrated by some of the board members [of LFP] and aimed, we are told, at ousting Korda. Resignations and new appointments had taken care of this internal friction' (Kulik, *Korda*, p. 120; see also Tabori, *Korda*, p. 139). Certainly by early 1935 neither Brownlow nor Dixey was listed among the directors of LFP on its stationery (see, for example, BFI, LFP Collection, C/1069/1).

33. Lejeune, 'The Private Lives of London Films; Part V', p. 98. For a sketch of Korda's relationship with Churchill in the 1930s, see D. J. Wenden, 'Churchill, Radio, and Cinema', pp. 215–39, esp. pp. 227–31. The abortive jubilee project would have been directed by Anthony Asquith and scripted by Churchill in collaboration with Biró and Wimperis. Asquith and Biró were to spend a fortnight with Churchill at Chartwell working on the script, an experience that reputedly left Biró 'dazzled' by the politician's ability to produce a complete script in 'two hours of continuous dictation'. 'There is no doubt about it,' the playwright is quoted as saying, 'a tremendous film-writer was lost in Churchill' (Lejeune, 'The Private Lives of London Films; Part V', p. 100). If the story is true, however, one wonders how the trio spent the remaining thirteen and a half days of the fortnight. Kulik suggests, more prosaically, that the trip involved Biró and Asquith 'giving Churchill instruction in the basics of script-writing' (Kulik, *Korda*, p. 255). Given that one of Churchill's suggestions, outlined in a letter to Korda, was that the signing of the 1922 Irish treaty be illustrated by a photograph of pre-war Cabinet ministers, animated, 'on the Mickey Mouse plan', it seems likely that he needed some advice on the practicalities of the medium (Gilbert [ed.], *Winston S. Churchill*, V, p. 562). Biró had, perhaps, imbibed something of Korda's capacity for producing quotable lines for press consumption.

34. Indeed, the director's close relationship with the Churchill administration after 1939 has led to the suggestion, first advanced by Ian Dalrymple, that it was the National Government which, at Churchill's urging, encouraged the Prudential Assurance to invest in London Films in the summer of 1934. But this idea has been effectively squashed by the detailed researches of Sarah Street in the Prudential archives, which have shown that it was commercial calculation rather than political pressure that prompted the Pru to invest (Street, 'Alexander Korda', pp. 164ff; Stockham, *The Korda Collection*, pp. 24–5).

35. For an account of these and other 'pacifist' films of the early to mid-1930s, see Richards, *The Age of the Dream Palace*, pp. 274–95. I differ from Richards here in interpreting *Things to Come* as a warning of the consequences of weakness in the face of foreign threat rather than as a pacifist film, and in seeing the argument for rearmament as implicit in all of Korda's 'political' films of the 1930s, rather than as suddenly adopted in 1937.

36. Ringer, 'Alexander Korda', p. 30.

37. Vincent Korda again provided the 'settings', and a number of the cast re-
    appeared, including Merle Oberon as a sultry Lady Blakeney, John Turnbull as
    Jellyband, and Gibb McLaughlin, who swapped his executioner's sword for a
    barber's razor but retained his curious 'French' accent.

38. The analogy was still more explicitly drawn in the sequel, *The Return of the
    Scarlet Pimpernel*, directed at Denham by Hans Schwartz (see Brunel, *Nice
    Work*, pp. 180–1; Kulik, *Korda*, p. 183).

39. *Richard II*, 3.i.150, in Wells and Taylor (eds), *The Oxford Shakespeare*, p. 375.

40. *The Spectator*, 3 November 1939, quoted in Kulik, *Korda*, p. 236.

41. Ibid., pp. 249–52.

42. M. Korda, *Charmed Lives*, p. 340; Stockham, *The Korda Collection*, p. 28. For the
    troubled history of the *Revolt in the Desert* project between 1934 and 1938, see
    Kulik, *Korda*, pp. 189–91.

43. Gough-Yates, 'Jews and Exiles in British Cinema', p. 535; Kulik, *Korda*, pp. 256ff;
    Stockham, *The Korda Collection*, p. 38. The most expansive claims for Korda's
    involvement in wartime espionage were made in Hyde, *Room 3603*. Korda's son
    Peter talked of his father's role as a 'secret courier' for Churchill during the war
    (Kulik, *Korda*, p. 256; M. Korda, *Charmed Lives*, pp. 152–7). For the 'Disraeli'
    jibe, see Tabori, *Korda*, p. 191.

5. MARRIAGE, SEX AND GENDER

1. For Oberon's early life and subsequent attempts to mythologise it, see Higham
   and Moseley, *Merle*; for an entertaining fictionalised treatment, see M. Korda,
   Queenie.

2. Mulvey, 'Visual Pleasure and Narrative Cinema', pp. 6–27.

3. Kulik, *Korda*, p. 92; Harper, *Picturing the Past*, p. 22.

4. *Private Life*, p. 43.

5. BFI Pressbook; *New York Times Film Reviews*, 13 November 1933, pp. 988–9.
   See also *Film Weekly*, 16 February 1934, p. 31 ('the humour [is] a little robust
   – not to say vulgar'), and 20 November 1933, p. 33 ('This is no sombre slab of
   English history, but a rollicking piece of lip-smacking, leg-whacking comedy
   – a bedroom and key-hole affair'). For Gamme, see *Film Weekly*, 20 October
   1933, p. 33. 'Women lost their heads over him: and such nice heads too!' drooled
   the publicity flyers (BFI Pressbook). See also Harper, *Picturing the Past*, p. 184;
   Callow, *Laughton*, p. 63. The slogan, from the *Chicago Tribune*, 26 April 1950,
   is cited in Street, 'Stepping Westward', pp. 51–62. It adapts London Films' own
   publicity strap-line, 'What a King! What a Lover! What a Man!', and its near
   alternative, 'What a king, what a man, what a lover!' (BFI Pressbook). The
   notion that the film could be marketed on the strength of its 'sexual' content
   was put most plainly in the trade magazine, the *Motion Picture Herald*, on 22
   September 1933, where it was claimed that 'there is room for wide-open selling
   and exploitation in the title and its indications of the Bluebeard of Kings who
   married six women and caused two of the six to pay for their infidelity ...

under the axe ... It's a costume piece, but only in the setting' (quoted in Macnab, *J. Arthur Rank*, p. 67).

6. *Private Life*, p. 38.

7. Kulik, *Korda*, p. 93.

8. Watts, 'Alexander Korda and the International Film', p. 14.

9. Kulik, *Korda*, pp. 91 and 94–5.

10. Low, *The History of the British Film, 1929–1939*, p. 58; Richards, *The Age of the Dream Palace*, p. 111.

11. The Board's report for 1929 condemned 'backstage dramas' that 'if not actually immoral, are at all events unmoral [sic] in practice and principle'. In its 1931 report the Board deplored the depiction in films 'of various phases of immorality and incidents which tend to bring the institution of marriage into contempt' (Richards, *The Age of the Dream Palace*, p. 93).

12. On the literary antecedents, see Walker, 'Laughable Men', pp. 1–15. In British film and television the tradition includes those obvious examples of inept manhood George Formby, Norman Wisdom, Charlie Drake and many of Kenneth Connor's roles in the *Carry On* films, through to, in more recent times, Ronnie Corbett's Timothy Lumsden in *Sorry*, Michael Crawford's Frank Spencer, both of the male roles in the Ronnie Barker and David Jason vehicle *Open All Hours*, and Jason's 'Del Boy' and Nicholas Lyndhurst's Rodney in the long-running BBC sitcom *Only Fools and Horses*. For a brilliant analysis of the 'adolescent sexuality' of George Formby's screen persona, which I gratefully draw upon here, see Richards, *The Age of the Dream Palace*, pp. 191–206.

13. The phrase is Kulik's, *Korda*, p. 92. See also ibid., p. 90.

14. Ibid., p. 90; Richards, *The Age of the Dream Palace*, p. 259. See, in this context, the astute comments in Street, *British National Cinema*, p. 40.

15. BFI Pressbook. See also Street, *British National Cinema*, p. 40; Harper, *Picturing the Past*, p. 22.

16. Kulik, *Korda*, p. 90; Harper, *Picturing the Past*, p. 27.

17. The role was initially assigned to an equally fictitious character named 'the earl of Stafford' (*Film Weekly*, 2 June 1933, p. 27).

18. Kulik, *Korda*, p. 90.

19. Street, *British National Cinema*, p. 41; *New York Times Film Reviews*, 13 November 1933, p. 989; Callow, *Laughton*, p. 61.

20. Harper, *Picturing the Past*, p. 21; Lejeune, 'The Private Lives of London Films', p. 82. See, for example, Freud, *On Sexuality*, Minsky (ed.), *Psychoanalysis and Gender*, esp. pp. 40ff.

21. In marital comedy the pre-adolescent metamorphoses into the henpecked husband by simply replacing the dominant mother with a dominant wife, continuing the essentials of their relationship intact. The characteristic theme of the relationship, his inadequacy, is simply expanded to include an overtly sexual dimension.

22. *Private Life*, p. 27. The Nurse's dominance in the bedchamber is emphasised by the removal from the final shooting script of the character of Mrs Barton,

who fulfilled a number of the basic duties concerning the royal bedlinen in the screenplay.

23. *Private Life*, pp. 38–9. The same point is reiterated later (p. 66) in the second exchange between Cornell and the Nurse over which of them has the right to prepare the royal bed, in which they argue over responsibility for the conception of the Prince of Wales. ('CORNELL: That was the King's doing. / NURSE: It was not! Did he get a son by his first wife? No! Did he get a son by his second wife? No! And why? Because you locked me out!')

24. Ibid., pp. 56–7ff.

25. Kulik, *Korda*, p. 91.

26. *Private Life*, p. 69.

27. Ibid., p. 51.

28. Le Touzel, 'The Woman Behind Charles Laughton', p. 7. For more on 'The Cave of Harmony', see Lanchester, *Charles Laughton and I*, pp. 49–58. It was precisely the exotic sexual quality that Lanchester brought to the role of Anne that was to lead to her casting two years later as that ultimate *femme fatale*, the eponymous female lead in James Whale's *Bride of Frankenstein* (Universal Pictures, 1935). Indeed, as Alberto Magnuel has noted, the later film nodded knowingly back to *Henry VIII* by including a figure strongly resembling Laughton's Henry among the homunculi that the sinister Dr Pretorius (Ernest Thesiger) shows to Henry Frankenstein (Colin Clive) in one of the film's campest scenes (Magnuel, *Bride of Frankenstein*, pp. 26 and 55).

29. *Private Life*, pp. 68–9.

30. Ibid., pp. 106–7.

31. Ibid., p. 108.

32. Kulik, *Korda*, pp. 45–6. Menelaus's rout takes on a further, class inflection, as it is a lower-status male, one of his household guards, with whom he chooses to undertake this exercise in homosocial bonding.

33. M. Korda, *Charmed Lives*, p. 117. For Laughton's difficulties with the role, see Callow, *Laughton*, pp. 113–22.

34. Kulik, *Korda*, p. 108. *Exit Don Juan* is the title used in much of the publicity material now in the BFI archive.

35. Kulik, *Korda*, p. 102; Harper, *Picturing the Past*, p. 24.

36. See, for example, *The Spectator*, 27 October 1933, and M. Korda, *Charmed Lives*, pp. 110ff. As John Gamme's review in *Film Weekly* shrewdly observed, Laughton's performance 'contrasts oddly with Korda's sober treatment of the historical background, and supplies most of the comedy in what can only be described as a tragi-comedy' (*Film Weekly*, 20 October 1933, p. 31).

37. *Private Life*, p. 9. The last line quoted was notably strengthened in the shooting script from the screenplay's more neutral 'You think she dies so that … ' to emphasise the consensus over Anne's innocence.

38. *Private Life*, p. 21. Note also the pointed contrast established between the dignity of Anne's last words, 'What a lovely day' (ibid.) and Jane Seymour's vacuous delivery of the same line in the succeeding shot. We are clearly intended to

side with Anne at this point and to appreciate the consequences of Henry's cruelty if not his responsibility for it.

6. FADE-OUT?

1. Frayling, *Things to Come*.
2. *Private Life*, pp. 49 and 9.
3. M. Korda, *Charmed Lives*, pp. 107 and 153; Tabori, *Korda*, p. 188.
4. This was a point picked up in Paul Rotha's review of *Catherine the Great*, in which he noted that 'It looks as if Bergner, Fairbanks, and the others have been given their heads, and the camera adjusted to them' (*Cinema Quarterly*, 2 [3], Spring 1934, pp. 186–7).

Sources

Addison, Paul, 'Patriotism Under Pressure: Lord Rothermere and British Foreign Policy', in G. Peele and C. Cook (eds), *The Politics of Reappraisal, 1918–1939* (London, 1975), pp. 189–208.

Ashton, H. S., *The Jew at Bay* (London, 1933).

Balcon, Michael, *Michael Balcon Presents ... A Lifetime of Films* (London, 1969).

Ball, Stuart (ed.), *Parliament and Politics in the Age of Baldwin and MacDonald: The Headlam Diaries, 1923–1935* (London, 1992).

Beard, Charles, 'Why Get It Wrong?', *Sight and Sound*, 2 (8), 1933–34, pp. 124–5.

Betts, E. (ed.), *The Private Life of Henry VIII* (London, 1934).

Brunel, Adrian, *Nice Work* (London, 1949).

Burnett, R. G. and E. D. Martell, *The Devil's Camera* (London, 1932).

Callow, Simon, *Charles Laughton: A Difficult Actor* (London, 1995).

Cesarani, David, 'Joynson-Hicks and the Racial Right in England after the First World War', in T. Kushner and K. Lunn (eds), *Traditions of Intolerance: Historical Perspectives on Fascism and Race Discourse in Britain* (Manchester, 1989), pp. 118–39.

Cheyette, Bryan, 'Jewish Stereotyping and English Literature 1875–1920: Towards a Political Analysis', in T. Kushner and K. Lunn (eds), *Traditions of Intolerance: Historical Perspectives on Fascism and Race Discourse in Britain* (Manchester, 1989).

Cohan, Steven, 'Case Study: Interpreting *Singing in the Rain*', in C. Gledhill and L. Williams (eds), *Reinventing Film Studies* (London, 2000), pp. 53–75.

Cole, Hubert, 'Henry VIII Blacks a Few Critical Eyes', *Film Weekly*, 16 February 1934, p. 11.

Collins Baker, C. H., *Catalogue of the Pictures at Hampton Court* (Glasgow, 1929).

Cousins, E. G., 'Charles Laughton at Elstree', *Picturegoer Weekly*, 10 June 1933.

—— 'On the British Sets', *Picturegoer Weekly*, 17 June 1933.

Dickinson, Margaret and Sarah Street (eds), *Cinema and State: The Film Industry and the Government, 1927–84* (London, 1985).

Eaton, Michael, *Chinatown* (London, 1997).

Eisner, Lotte H., *The Haunted Screen* (London, 1969).

Frayling, Christopher, *Things to Come* (London, 1995).

Freud, Sigmund, *On Sexuality*, Penguin Freud Library, Vol. 7 (Harmondsworth, 1991).

Gaines, Jane M., 'Dream/Factory', in R. Gledhill and X. Williams (eds), *Reinventing Film Studies* (London, 2000), pp. 100–13.

Gilbert, Martin (ed.), *Winston S. Churchill: Companion*, Vol. V (London, 1981).

Gough-Yates, Kevin, 'The European Film Maker in Exile in Britain, 1933–1945', Unpublished PhD thesis, Open University, 1990.

— 'Jews and Exiles in British Cinema', in *The Leo Baeck Institute Yearbook* (1992).

Greenhalgh, Paul, *Ephemeral Vistas: The Expositions Universelles, Great Exhibitions and World Fairs, 1851–1939* (Manchester, 1988).

Hamilton, D. (ed.), *A Chronicle of England During the Reigns of the Tudors*, 2 vols (Oxford, 1875).

Harper, Sue, *Picturing the Past: The Rise and Fall of the British Costume Film* (London, 1994).

Higham, Charles, *Charles Laughton: An Intimate Biography* (London, 1976).

Higham, Charles and Roy Moseley, *Merle: A Biography of Merle Oberon* (Sevenoaks, 1983).

Hollins, T. J., 'The Conservative Party and Film Propaganda Between the Wars', *English Historical Review*, XCVI, 1981, pp. 359–69.

Hyde, H. Montgomery, *Room 3606: The Story of the British Intelligence Centre in New York During World War II* (New York, 1962).

Ives, E. W., *Anne Boleyn* (Oxford, 1986).

Korda, Alexander, 'Costume Films Have Brought New Life to the Screen', *Film Weekly*, 4 May 1934, p. 19.

Korda, Michael, *Charmed Lives: A Family Romance* (London, 1980).

— *Queenie* (London, 1986).

Kulik, Karol, *Alexander Korda: The Man Who Could Work Miracles* (London, 1975).

Kushner, Tony and Kenneth Lunn (eds), *Traditions of Intolerance: Historical Perspectives on Fascism and Race Discourse in Britain* (Manchester, 1989).

Lamb, Richard, *The Drift to War, 1922–1939* (London, 1989).

Lanchester, Elsa, *Charles Laughton and I* (London and New York, 1938).

Lane, A. H., *The Alien Menace*, 3rd edn (London, 1932).

Lejeune, C. A., 'The Private Lives of London Films', *Nash's Pall Mall Magazine*, September 1936, pp. 78–85.

— 'The Private Life of London Films; Part V', *Nash's Pall Mall Magazine*, January 1937, pp. 96–104.

Le Touzel, Anthony, 'The Woman Behind Charles Laughton', *Film Weekly*, 3, November 1933, p. 7.

Lindsay, Philip, 'The Camera Turns to History', *Cinema Quarterly*, 2 (1), 1933, pp. 10–11.

Lockhart, Freda Bruce, 'Is He Really Alexander the Great?', *Film Pictorial*, 26 October 1935.

Low, Rachael, *The History of British Film, 1929–1939: Film Making in 1930s Britain* (London, 1985).

Macnab, Geoffrey, *J. Arthur Rank and the British Film Industry* (London, 1993).

Magnuel, Alberto, *Bride of Frankenstein* (London, 1997).

Mikes, George, *How to be a Brit* (Harmondsworth, 1987).

Minsky, R. (ed.), *Psychoanalysis and Gender: An Introductory Reader* (London, 1996).

Mulvey, Laura, 'Visual Pleasure and Narrative Cinema', *Screen*, 16, 1975, pp. 6–27.

Oakley, C., *Where We Came In: Seventy Years of the British Film Industry* (London, 1964).

Richards, Jeffrey, *The Age of the Dream Palace: Cinema and Society in Britain, 1930–1939* (London, 1984).

Ringer, Paula, 'Alexander Korda: Producer, Director, Propagandist', *Classic Images*, 1995, pp. 30–2 and C1–C2.

Rotha, Paul, 'Review of *Catherine the Great*', *Cinema Quarterly*, 2 (3), Spring 1934, pp. 186–7.

Sedgwick, John, 'Cinema-going Preferences in Britain in the 1930s', in J. Richards (ed.), *The Unknown 1930s: An Alternative History of the British Cinema* (London, 1998), pp. 1–35.

Stevenson, John, 'The Politics of Violence', in G. Peele and C. Cook (eds), *The Politics of Reappraisal, 1918–1939* (London, 1975), pp. 146–56.

Stockham, Martin, *The Korda Collection* (London, 1992).

Street, Sarah, 'Alexander Korda, Prudential Assurance, and British Film Finance in the 1930s', *Historical Journal of Film, Radio and Television*, 6, 1986, p. 161–79.

— *British National Cinema* (London, 1997).

— 'Stepping Westward: The Distribution of British Films in America and the Case of *The Private Life of Henry VIII*', in J. Ashby and A. Higson (eds), *British Cinema, Past and Present* (London 2000), pp. 51–62.

Tabori, Paul, *Alexander Korda* (New York, 1959).

Tallents, Stephen, *The Projection of England* [1932] (London, 1955).

Taylor, Philip M., *The Projection of Britain: British Overseas Publicity and Propaganda, 1919–1939* (Cambridge, 1981).

— 'British Official Attitudes Towards Propaganda Abroad', in N. Pronay and D. W. Spring (eds), *Propaganda, Politics and Film, 1918–45* (London, 1982), pp. 23–49.

Thompson, Neville, *The Anti-Appeasers: Conservative Opposition to Appeasement in the 1930s* (Oxford, 1971).

Vasudevan, Ravi S., 'The Politics of Cultural Address in a "Transitional" Cinema: A Case Study of Indian Popular Cinema', in R. Gledhill and L. Williams (eds), *Reinventing Film Studies* (London, 2000), pp. 130–64.

Walker, Greg, 'Laughable Men: Comedy and Masculinity from Chaucer to Shakespeare', in R. Mullini (ed.), *Theta*, VI (Leiden, 2002), pp. 1–15.

Watts, Stephen, 'Filming the King of Many Wives', *Film Weekly*, 2 June 1933.

— 'Alexander Korda and the International Film', *Cinema Quarterly*, 2, August, pp. 12–15.

Wells, S. and G. Taylor (eds), *The Oxford Shakespeare: The Complete Works* (Oxford, 1999).

Wenden, D. J., 'Churchill, Radio, and Cinema', in R. Blake and W. R. Louis (eds), *Churchill* (Oxford, 1993), pp. 215–39.

Williamson, Philip, *Stanley Baldwin: Conservative Leadership and National Values* (Cambridge, 1999).

Wood, Alan, *Mr Rank: A Study of J. Arthur Rank and British Films* (London, 1952).

Young, K. (ed.), *The Diaries of Sir Robert Bruce Lockhart*, 2 vols (Basingstoke, 1973).